1930s

Ten Years of Popular Hits Arranged for EASY PIANO

Arranged by Dan Coates

DECADE by DECADE

Alfred

Contents

ANYTHING GOES

Cole Porter's 1934 show *Anything Goes* has been revived multiple times, released twice on film, and is a popular choice for school and community theater productions. This was the first Porter show to feature Ethel Merman, the "Grande Dame of the Broadway Stage" who would star in five of his musicals. Porter loved her loud, brassy voice, and wrote many numbers that highlighted her strengths.

Words and Music by Cole Porter
Arranged by Dan Coates

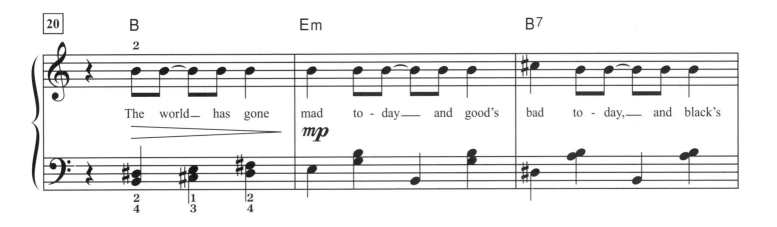

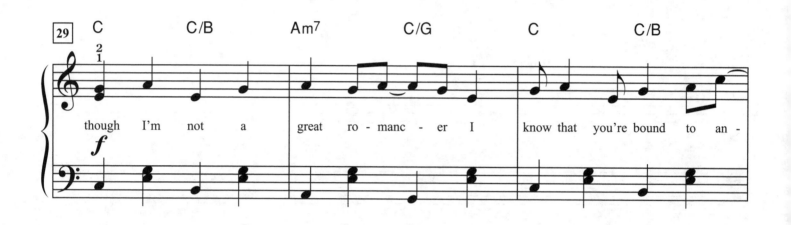

ARE YOU HAVIN' ANY FUN?

Sammy Fain was one of the most prolific composers of mid-20th century popular song. He received nine Academy Award nominations and won twice: "Secret Love" (1953) and "Love Is a Many-Splendored Thing" (1955). Fain also composed scores for television and for Walt Disney films. Jack Yellen wrote the lyrics to countless popular songs in the Great American Songbook and was also a writer for Sophie Tucker, the famous vaudevillian performer.

Lyrics by Jack Yellen
Music by Sammy Fain
Arranged by Dan Coates

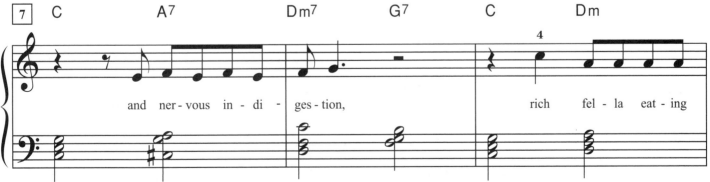

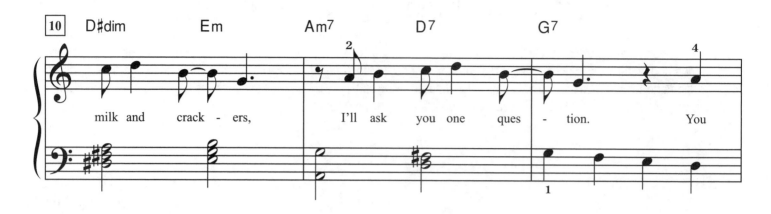

milk and crack - ers, I'll ask you one ques - tion. You

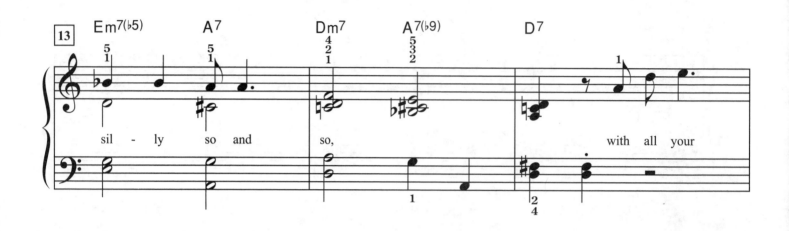

sil - ly so and so, with all your

dough: Are you hav - in' an - y fun? What-cha get - tin' out - ta

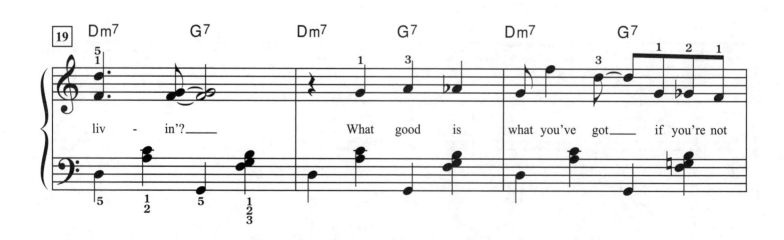

liv - in'?____ What good is what you've got____ if you're not

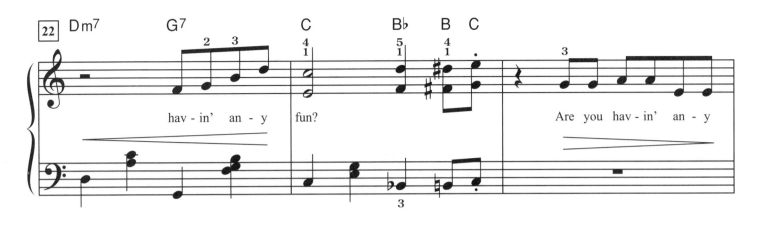

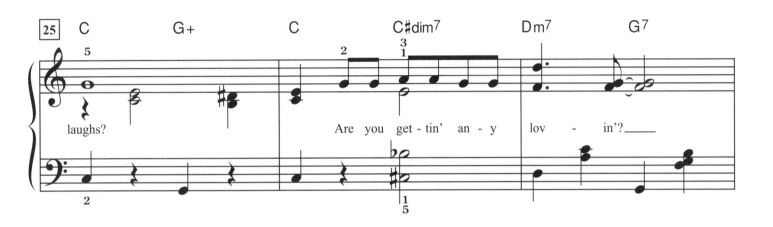

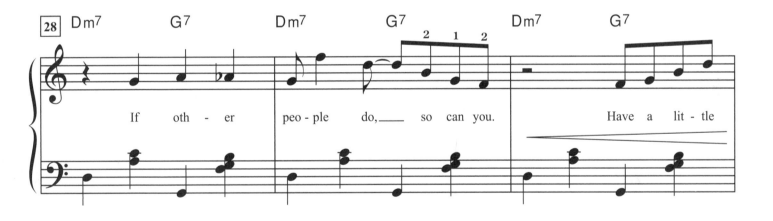

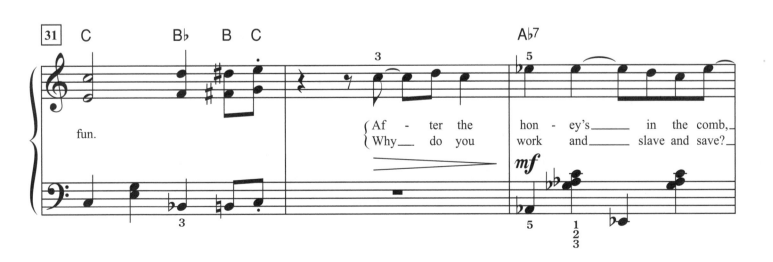

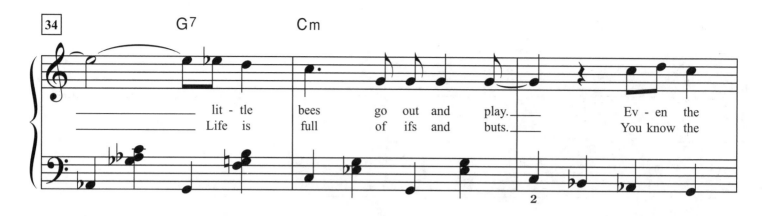

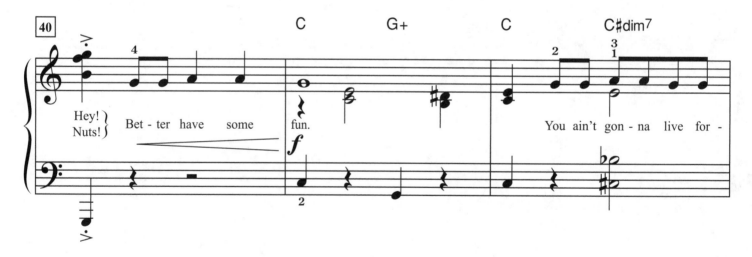

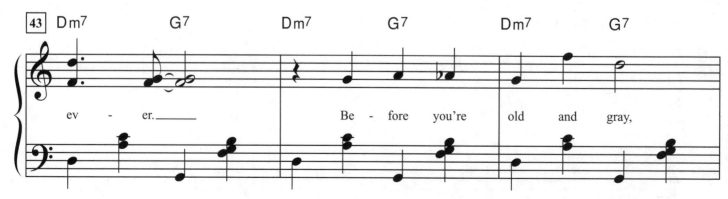

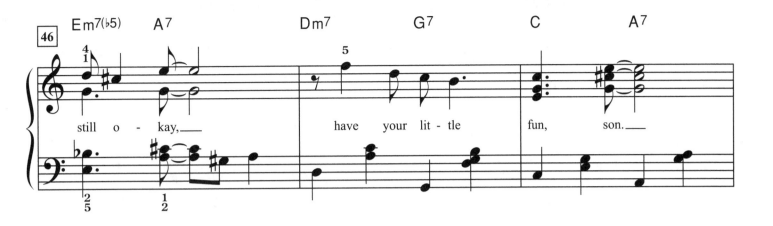

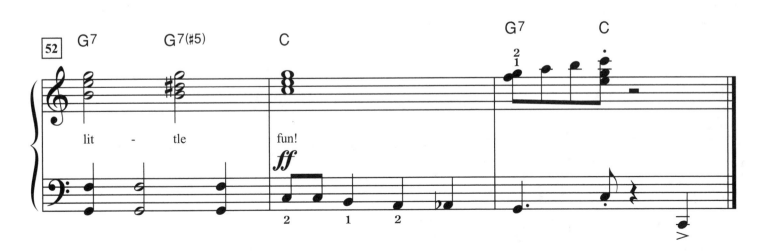

BEGIN THE BEGUINE

The *beguine* is a ballroom dance similar to the rumba. The dance inspired Cole Porter's "Begin the Beguine," which was first introduced in the 1935 Broadway musical *Jubilee*. The song gained popularity in 1938 when Artie Shaw's Orchestra recorded an extended version, and many others—Benny Goodman, Glenn Miller, Tommy Dorsey, Frank Sinatra, Ella Fitzgerald—would also record this standard.

Words and Music by Cole Porter
Arranged by Dan Coates

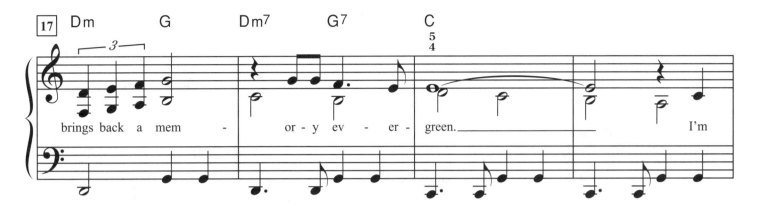

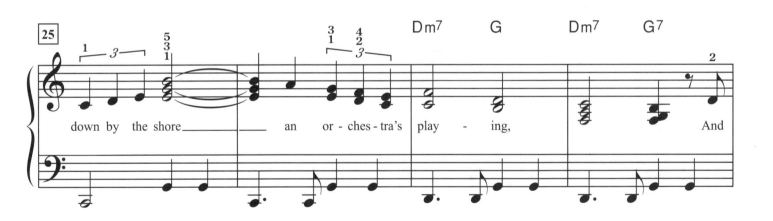

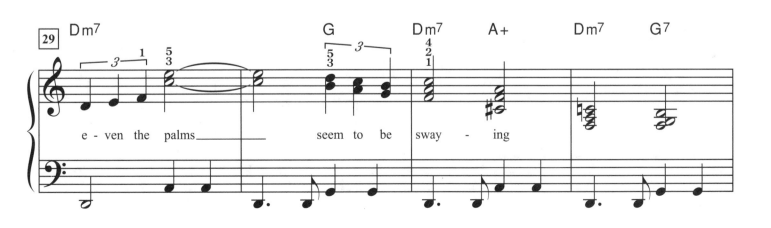

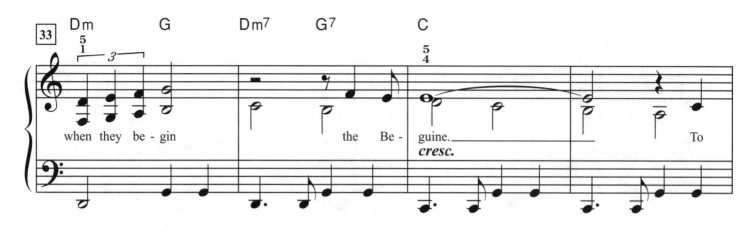

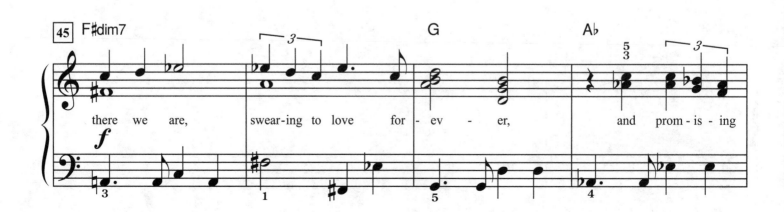

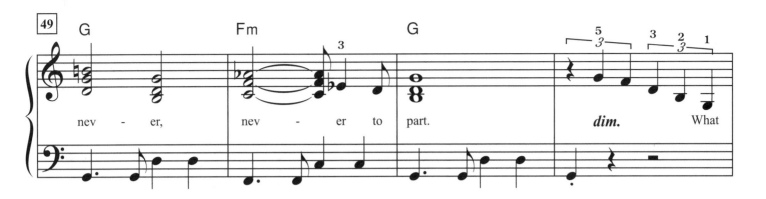

never, never to part. *dim.* What

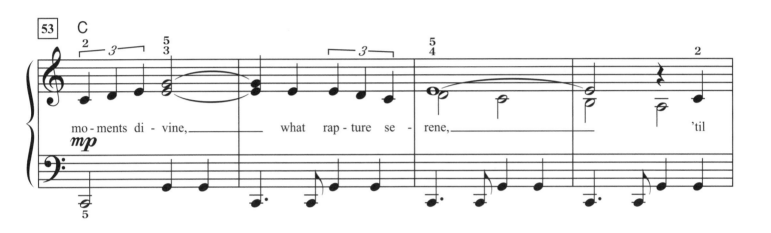

moments divine, what rapture serene, 'til

clouds came along to disperse the joys we had tasted and

now when I hear people curse the chance that was wasted, I

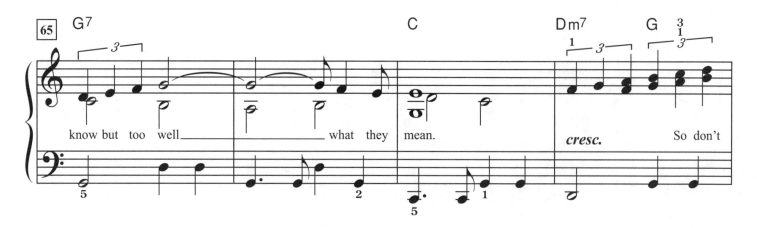

know but too well _____ what they mean. *cresc.* So don't

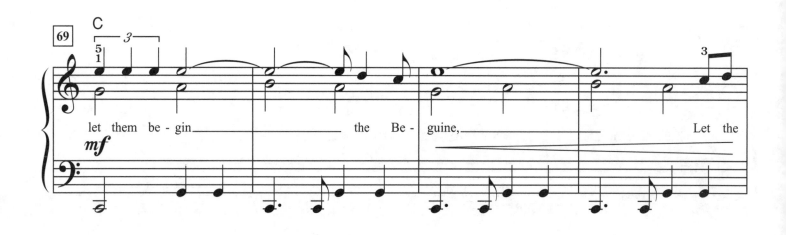

let them be - gin _____ the Be - guine, _____ Let the
mf

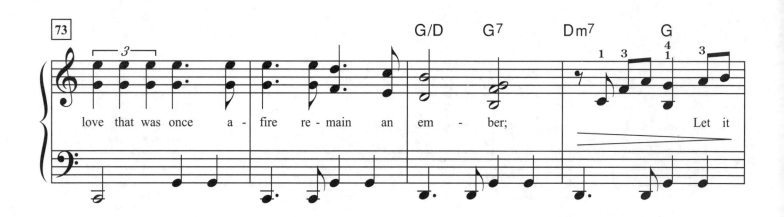

love that was once a - fire re - main an em - ber; Let it

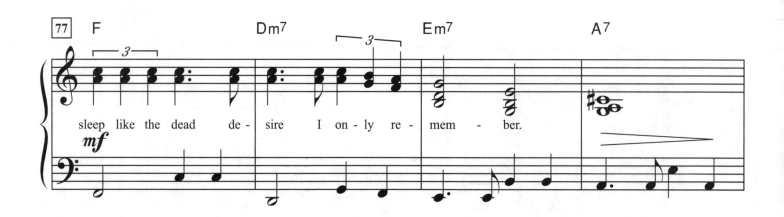

sleep like the dead de - sire I on - ly re - mem - ber.
mf

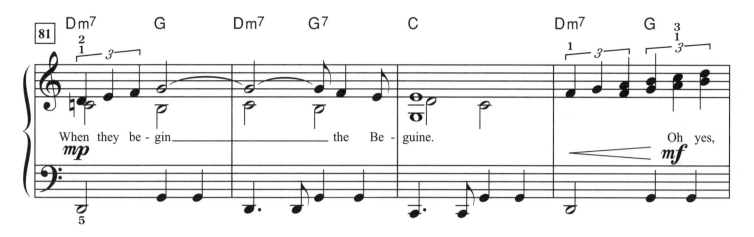

When they be - gin _____ the Be - guine. Oh yes,

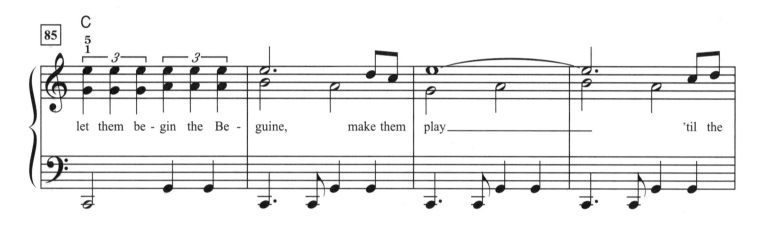

let them be - gin the Be - guine, make them play _____ 'til the

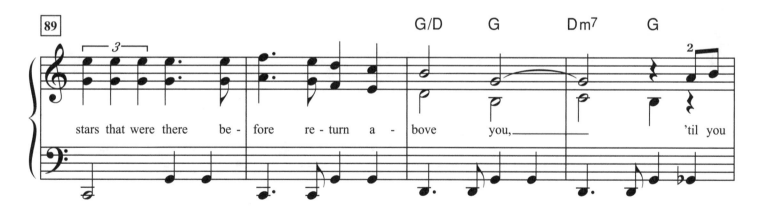

stars that were there be - fore re - turn a - bove you, _____ 'til you

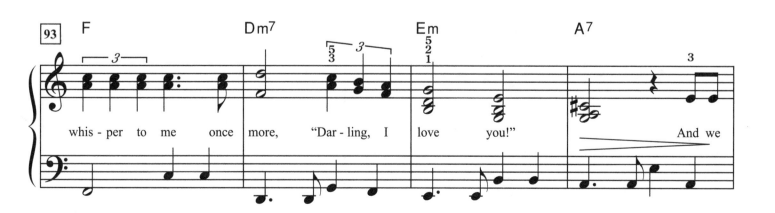

whis - per to me once more, "Dar - ling, I love you!" And we

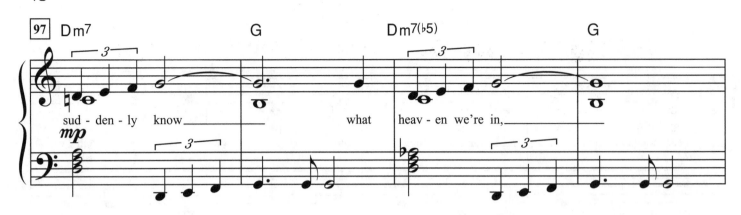

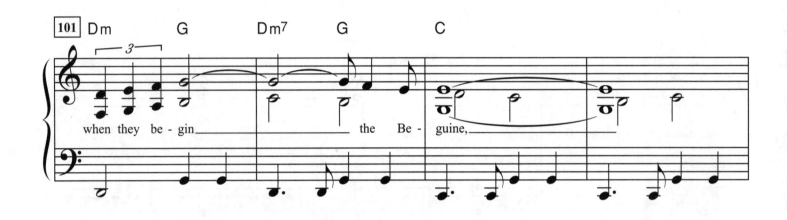

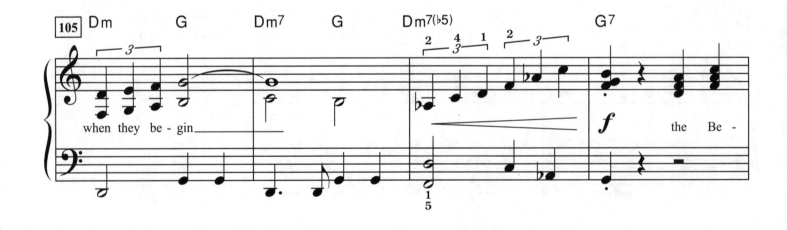

BILL BAILEY, WON'T YOU PLEASE COME HOME

Originally from Detroit, Michigan, Hughie Cannon was a pianist and a vaudeville and jazz composer. "Bill Bailey, Won't You Please Come Home" is his best-known composition and has been performed by a wide array of artists including Patsy Cline, Bobby Darin, Phish, Michael Bublé, and many others.

Words and Music by Hughie Cannon
Arranged by Dan Coates

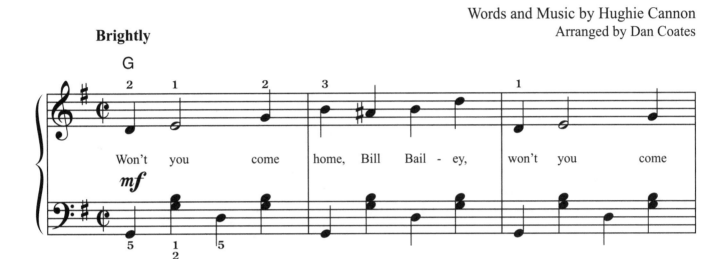

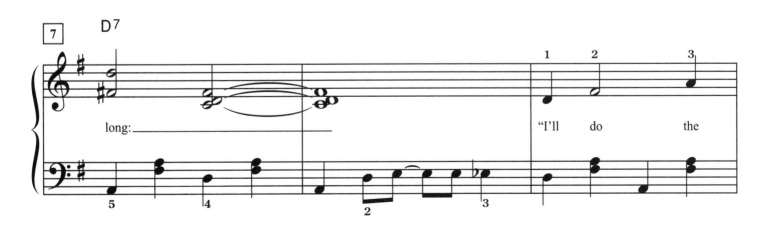

cook - ing, dar - ling, I'll pay de rent,

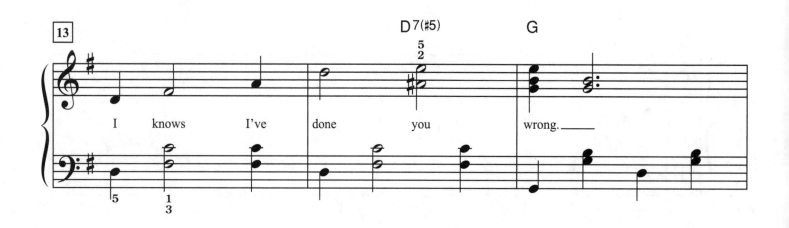

I knows I've done you wrong.____

'Mem - ber dat rain - y eve dat

I drove you out, wid noth - in' but a

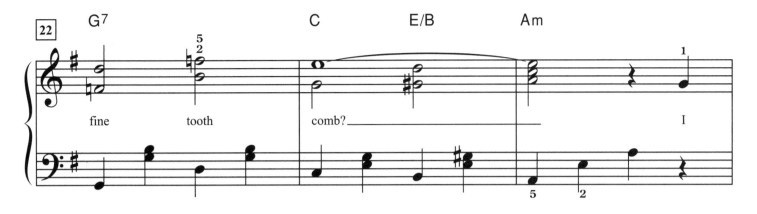

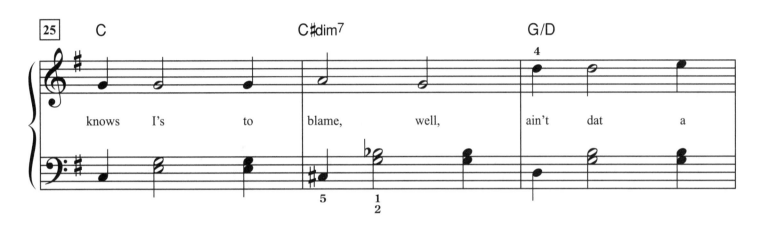

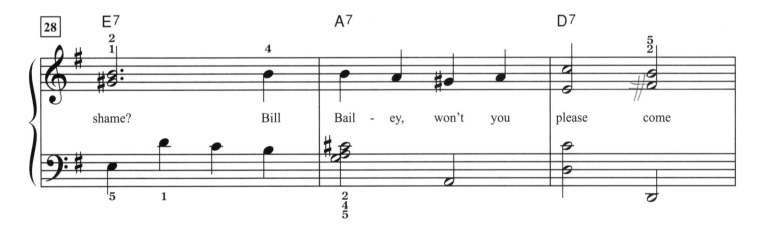

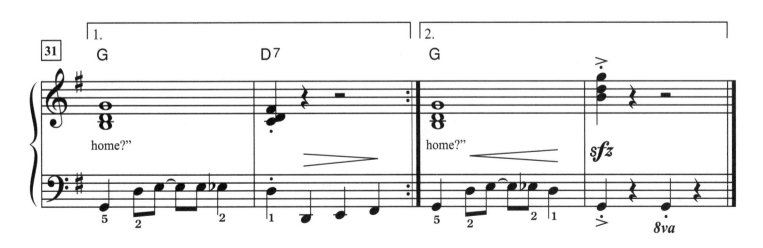

BLUE MOON

Though "Blue Moon" was penned in 1934 by Richard Rodgers and Lorenz Hart, perhaps the most famous version is the 1961 recording by The Marcels, a doo-wop group from Pittsburgh, Pennsylvania. Their up-tempo rendering of this classic ballad garnered a #1 hit, sold over a million copies, and earned a spot on the Rock and Roll Hall of Fame's "500 Songs that Shaped Rock and Roll" list.

Music by Richard Rodgers
Lyrics by Lorenz Hart
Arranged by Dan Coates

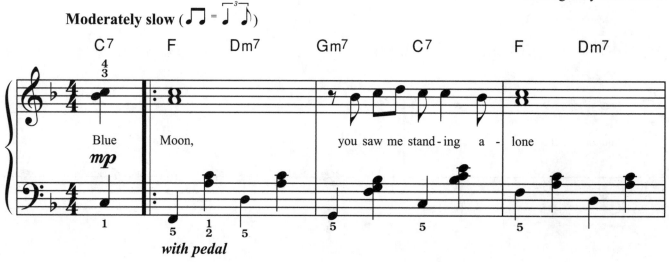

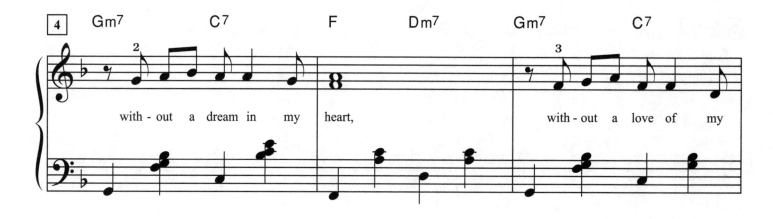

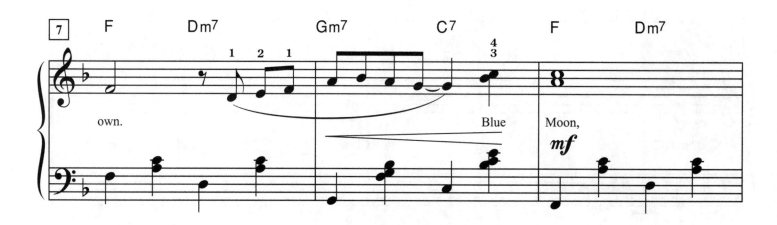

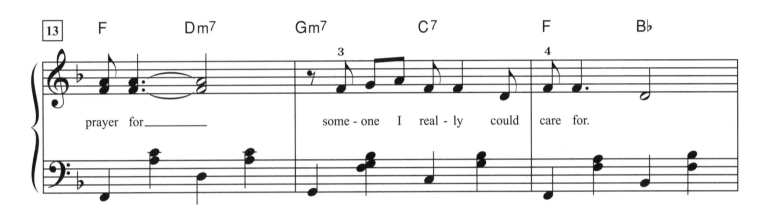

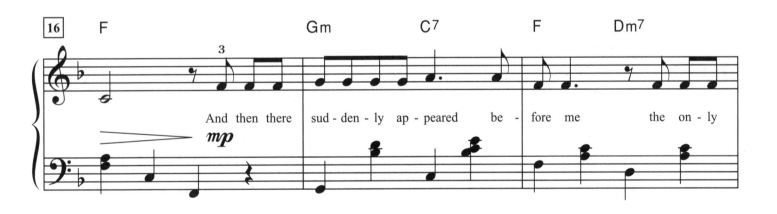

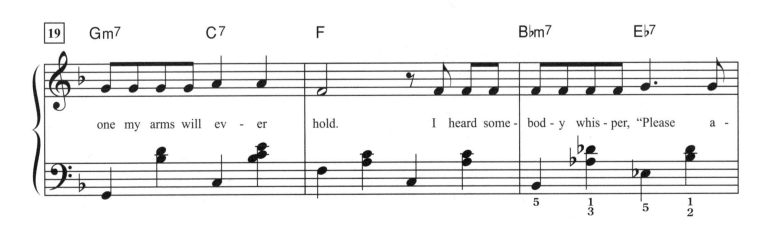

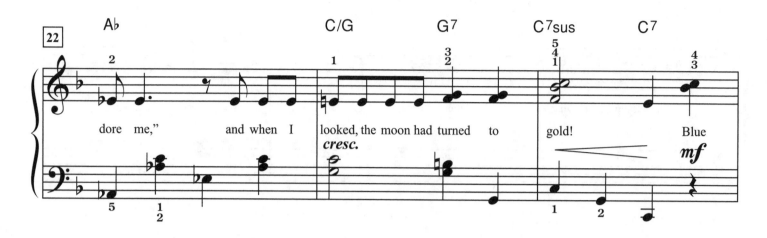

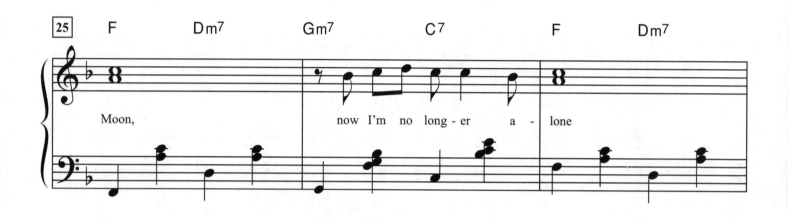

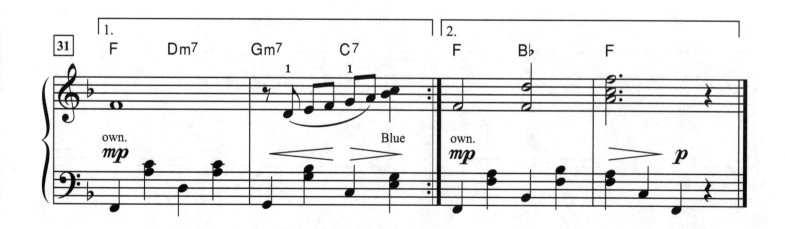

THE BOULEVARD OF BROKEN DREAMS

"The Boulevard of Broken Dreams" was first performed in the 1934 film *Moulin Rouge* starring Constance Bennett and directed by Sidney Lanfield. Sixteen years later, legendary crooner Tony Bennett would get lucky with the song. His demo recording of it sparked a contract with Columbia Records—his first and career-launching record deal.

Words by Al Dubin
Music by Harry Warren
Arranged by Dan Coates

13 Dm7(♭5)   G7   Dm7(♭5)   G7

schemes.   And gig-o-lo and__ gig-o-lette wake up to find their eyes are

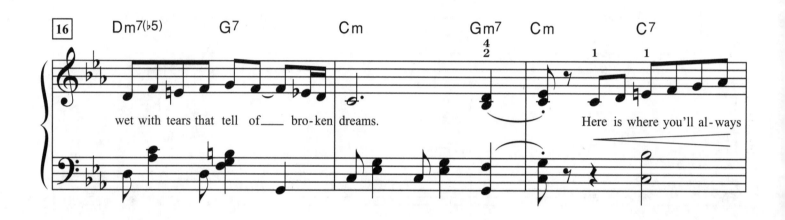

16 Dm7(♭5)   G7   Cm   Gm7   Cm   C7

wet with tears that tell of__ bro-ken dreams.   Here is where you'll al-ways

19 Gm7(♭5)   C7   Fm

find   me,   al-ways walk-ing up and   down.

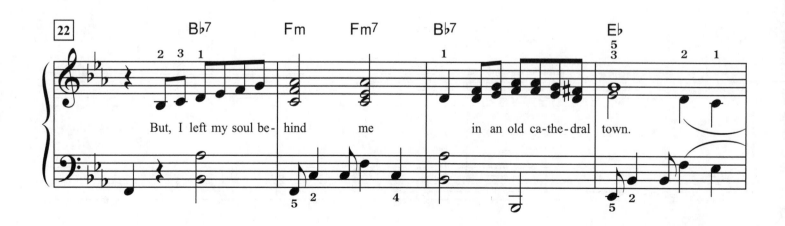

22 B♭7   Fm   Fm7   B♭7   E♭

But, I left my soul be- hind   me   in an old ca-the-dral town.

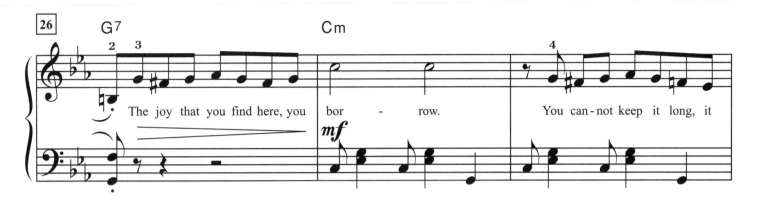

The joy that you find here, you bor - row. You can - not keep it long, it

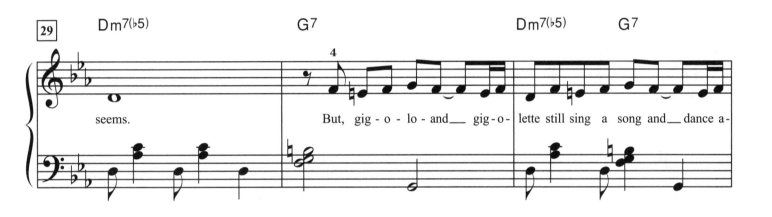

seems. But, gig - o - lo - and__ gig - o - lette still sing a song and__ dance a-

1.

long the bou - le - vard of bro - ken dreams. Here is where you'll al - ways

2.

long the bou - le - vard of bro - ken dreams.

BUT NOT FOR ME

"But Not for Me" was written for George and Ira Gershwin's 1930 musical *Girl Crazy*, the show that made stars out of both Ginger Rogers and Ethel Merman. Other notable songs from *Girl Crazy* include "I Got Rhythm" (page 65) and "Embrace-able You" (page 37). "But Not for Me" has been used in many movies including *When Harry Met Sally*, *Manhattan*, and *Four Weddings and a Funeral*, to name a few.

Music and Lyrics by
George Gershwin and Ira Gershwin
Arranged by Dan Coates

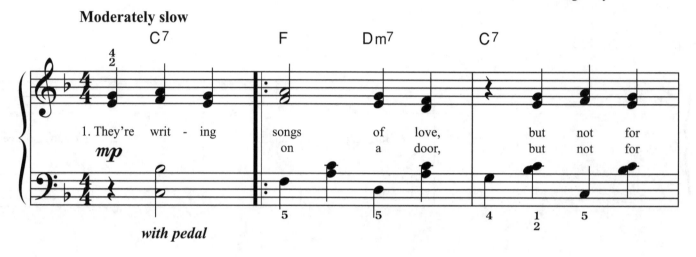

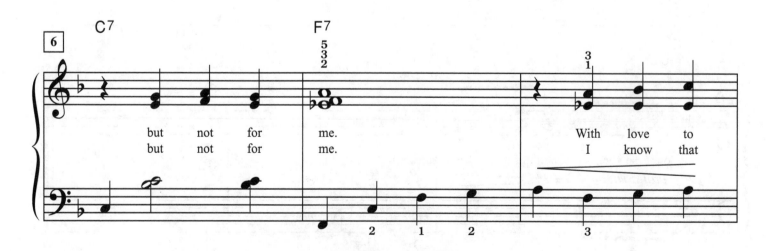

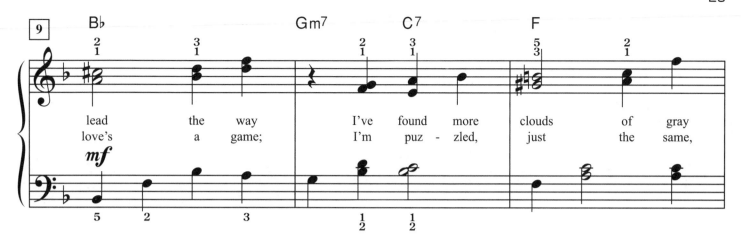

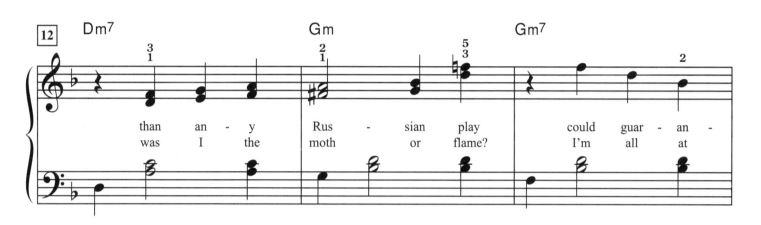

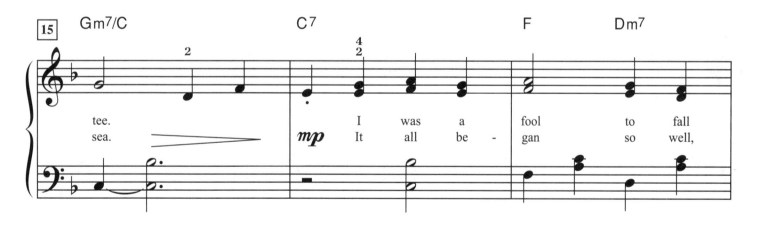

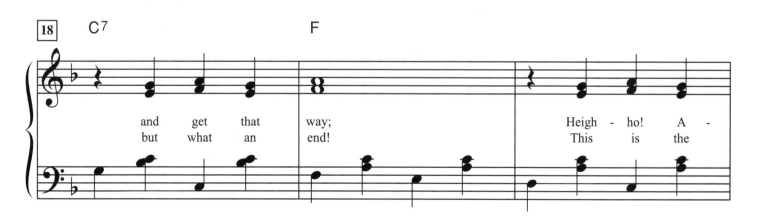

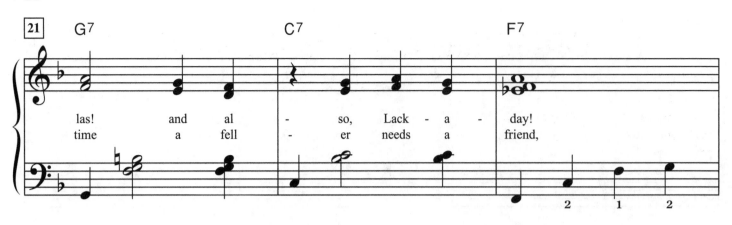

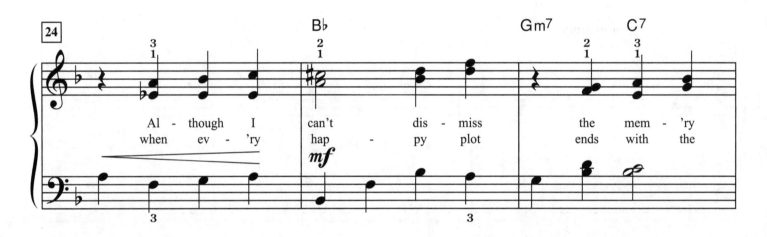

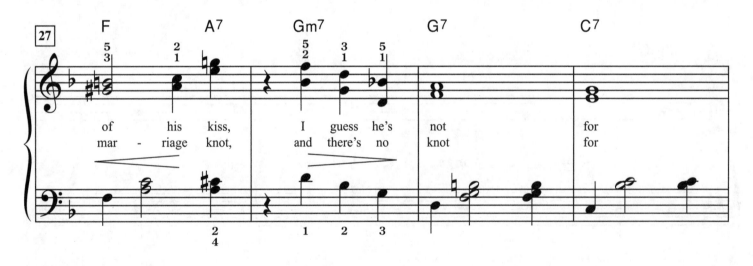

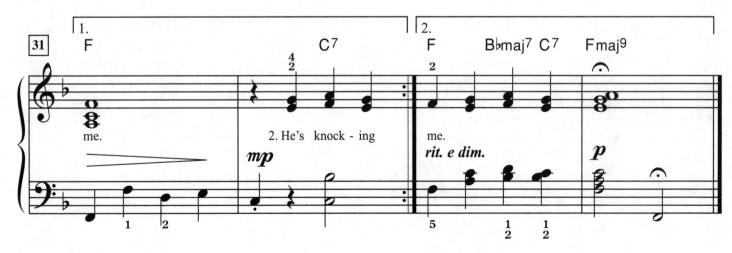

DANCING ON THE CEILING

The 1930 Rodgers and Hart musical *Evergreen,* starring Jessie Matthews and Sonnie Hale, was a great success, running for 254 performances in London where it premiered. In the show, the production number for "Dancing on the Ceiling" featured a revolving stage on which the two main characters danced around a chandelier, which was meant to suggest the ceiling. In 1934 *Evergreen* was adapted into a movie, which also starred Matthews who continued to grow in popularity as an actress and dancer.

Words by Lorenz Hart
Music by Richard Rodgers
Arranged by Dan Coates

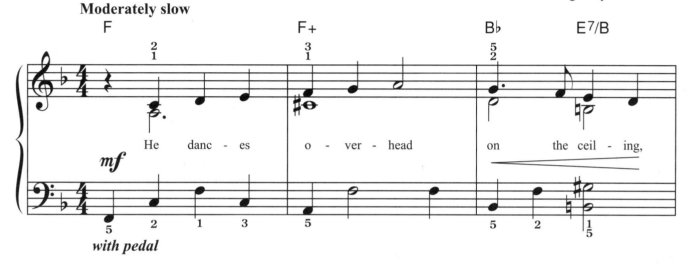

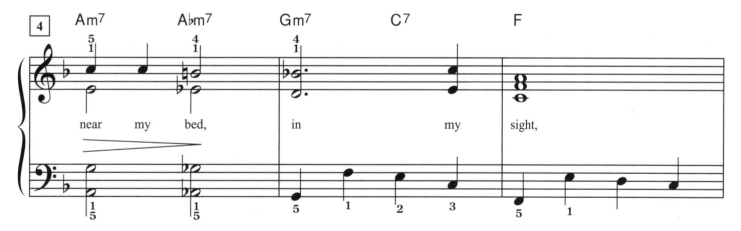

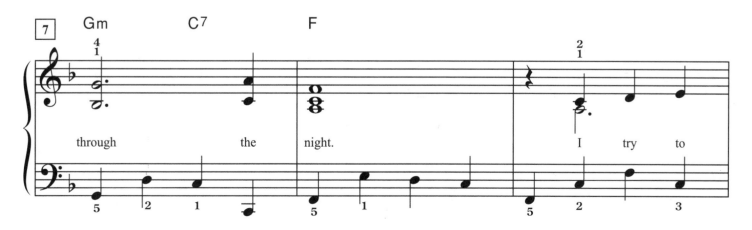

EASY TO LOVE

"Easy to Love" was written for the 1936 MGM musical film *Born to Dance*, starring Eleanor Powell, James (Jimmy) Stewart, Virginia Bruce, Buddy Ebsen and Frances Langford. In addition to "Easy to Love," "I've Got You Under My Skin" (page 93) was also featured in the film and received an Academy Award nomination for Best Song.

Words and Music by Cole Porter
Arranged by Dan Coates

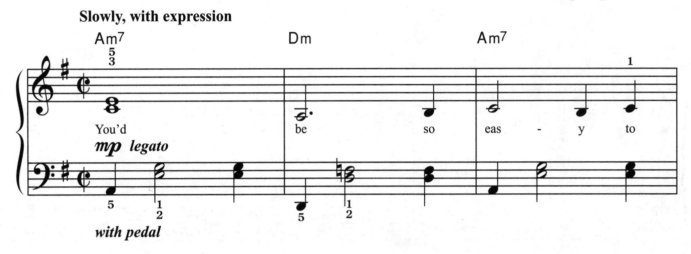

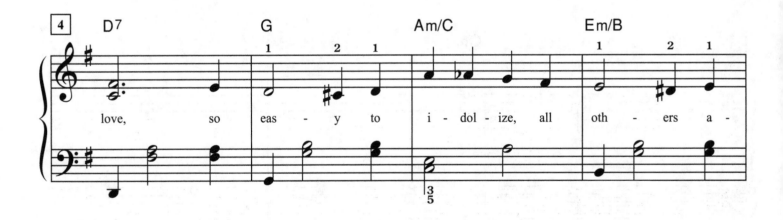

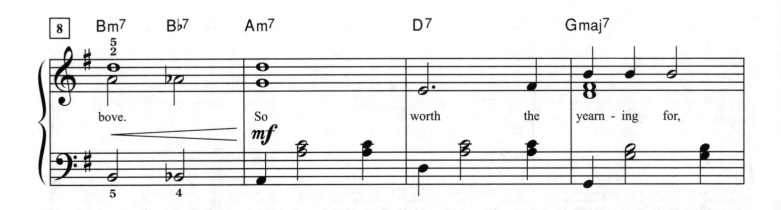

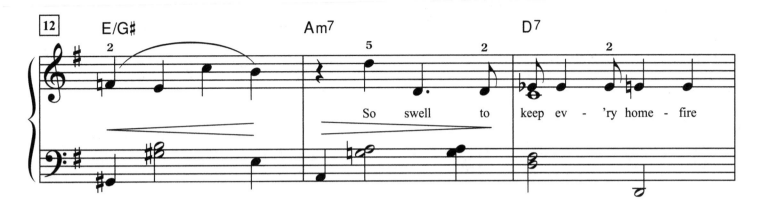

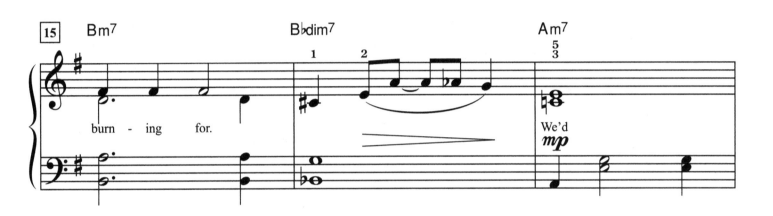

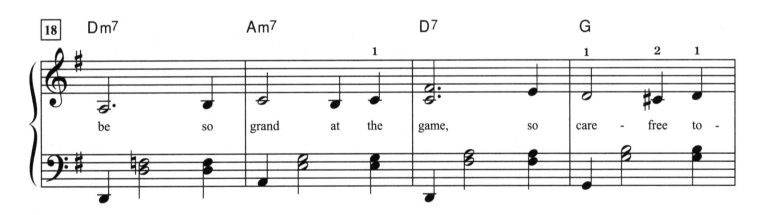

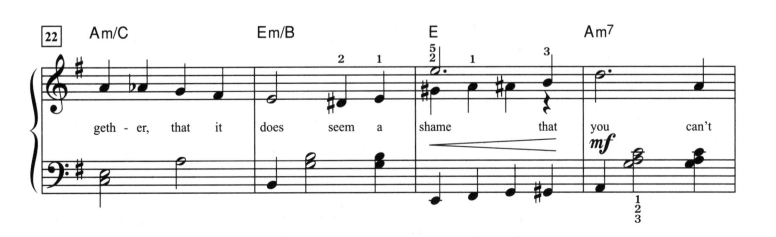

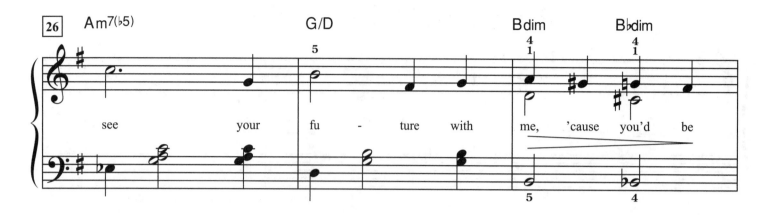

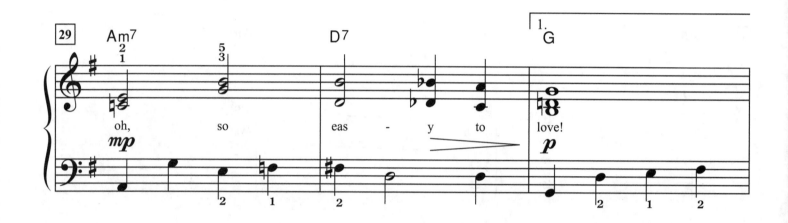

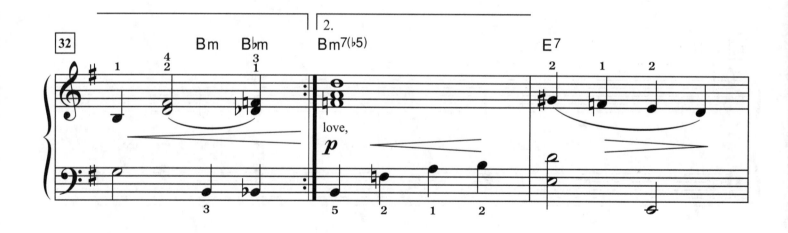

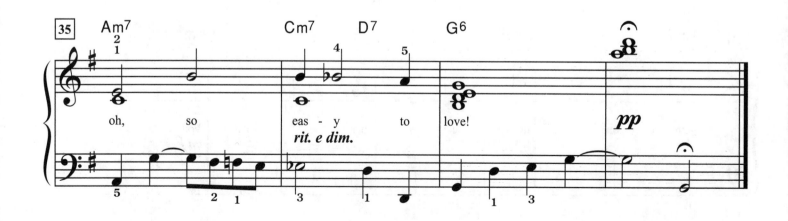

EMBRACEABLE YOU

"Embraceable You" was published in 1930 and was featured in the hit musical *Girl Crazy*. Ginger Rogers performed the song in the show gliding through a routine choreographed by her iconic dance partner Fred Astaire. Other hit songs from *Girl Crazy* include "I Got Rhythm" (page 65) and "But Not for Me" (page 28).

Music and Lyrics by
George Gershwin and Ira Gershwin
Arranged by Dan Coates

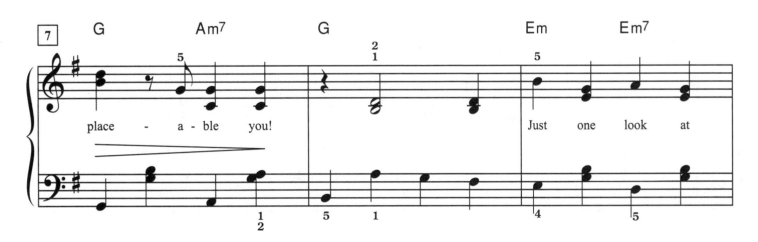

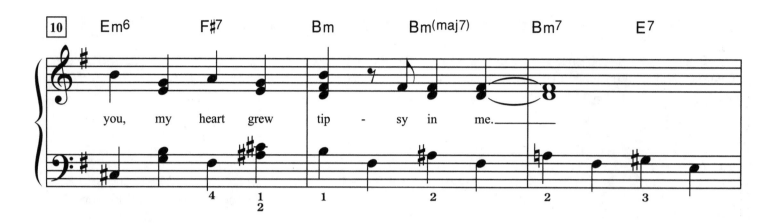

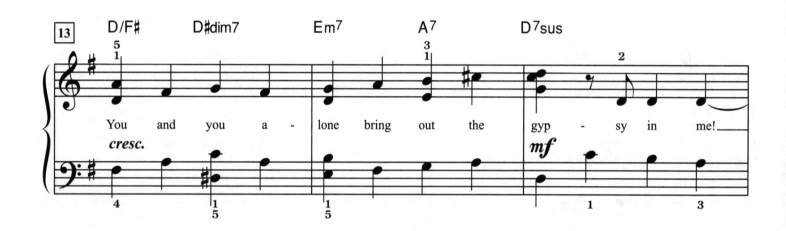

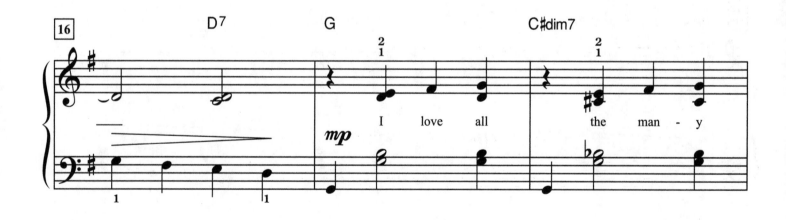

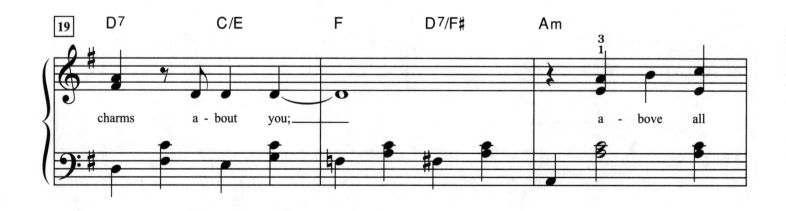

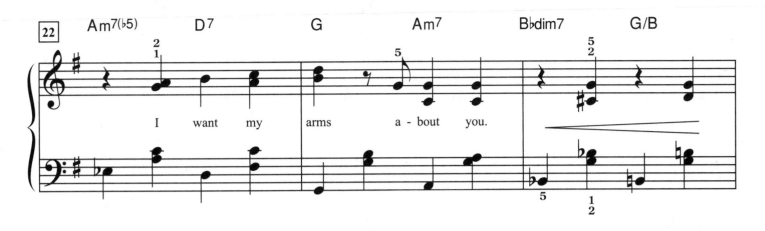

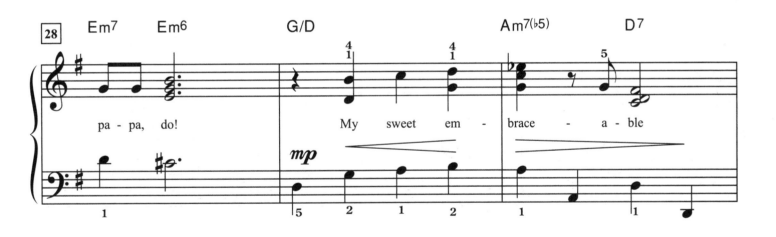

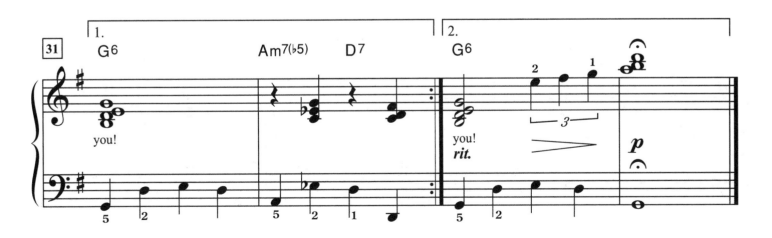

FALLING IN LOVE WITH LOVE

"Falling In Love with Love" is from the 1938 Rodgers and Hart musical *The Boys from Syracuse.* The show's plot is based on Shakespeare's *The Comedy of Errors,* which involves two sets of twins who are separated as children and the antics that ensue when their friends and families mistake their identities. In 1940, a movie version of the musical was released that was nominated for two Academy Awards.

Words by Lorenz Hart
Music by Richard Rodgers
Arranged by Dan Coates

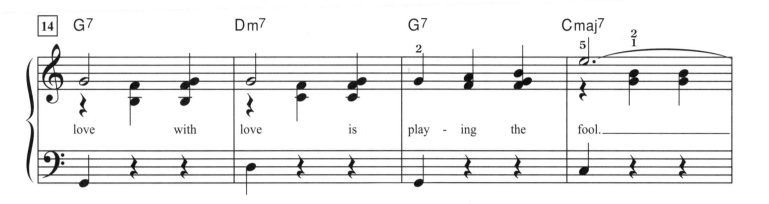

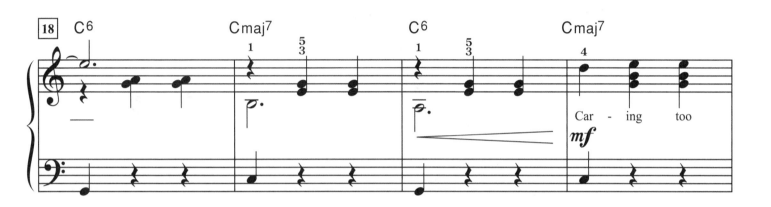

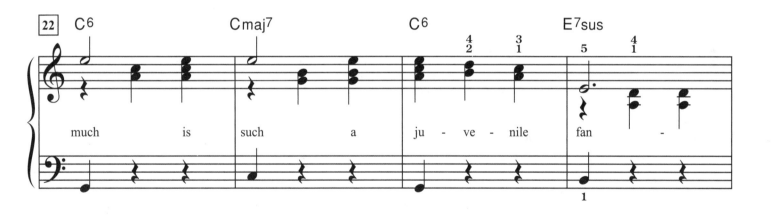

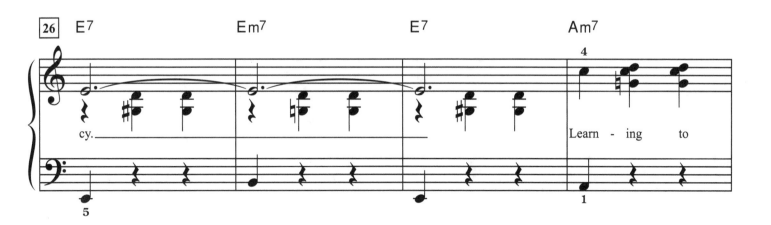

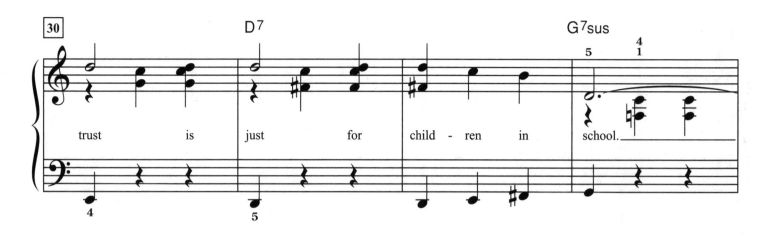

trust   is   just   for   child - ren   in   school.

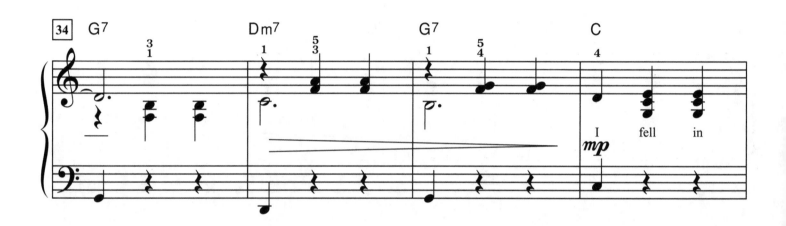

I   fell   in

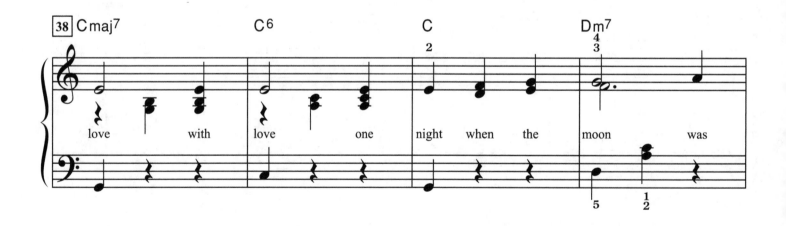

love   with   love   one   night   when   the   moon   was

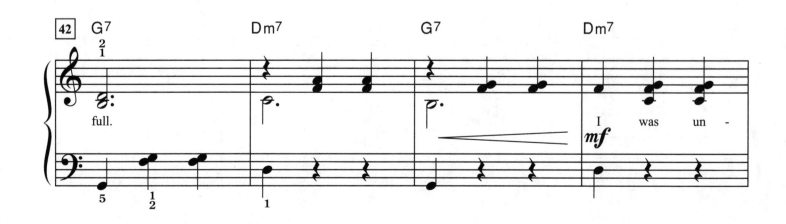

full.   I   was   un -

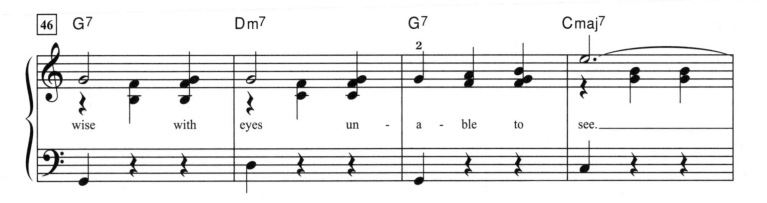

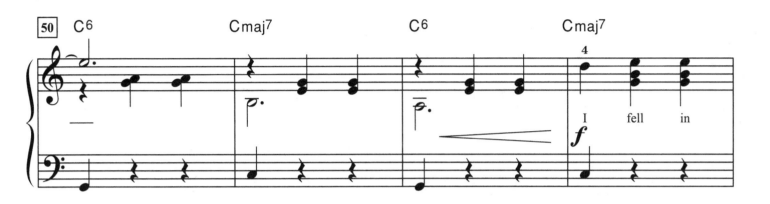

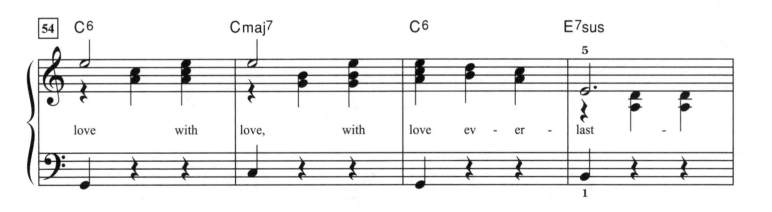

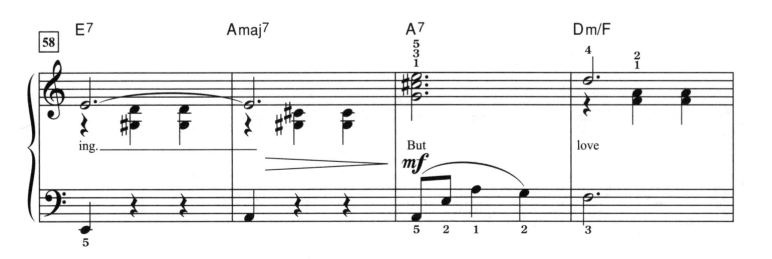

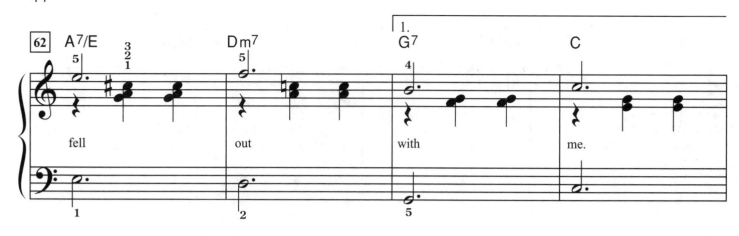

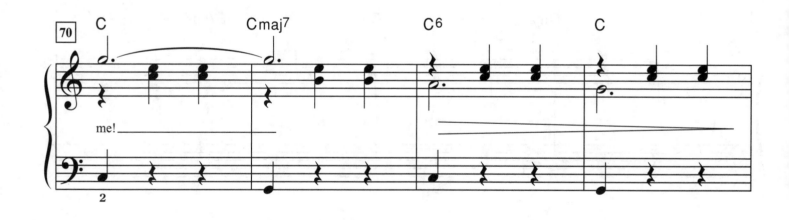

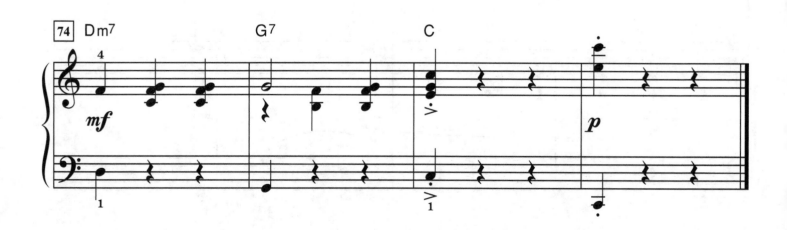

THE GOLD DIGGERS' SONG
(WE'RE IN THE MONEY)

This famous tune was originally used in the 1933 movie *42nd Street*. However, it is commonly associated with the Broadway musical of the same name, which opened in 1980 and ran for 3,486 performances before closing in 1989. It was revived in 2001 and earned Tony Awards for Best Revival and for Best Actress in a Musical (Christine Ebersole). The song from Al Dubin and Harry Warren's catchy score is widely used today and considered an American classic.

Lyrics by Al Dubin
Music by Harry Warren
Arranged by Dan Coates

Brightly

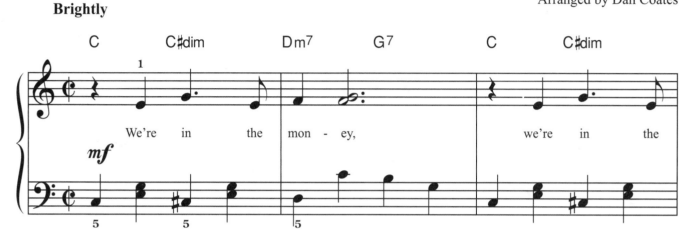

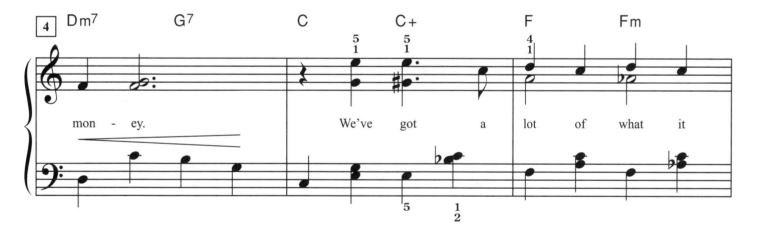

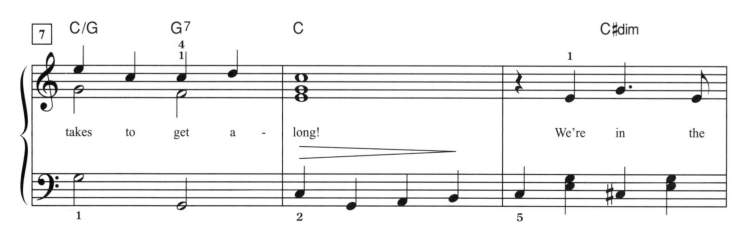

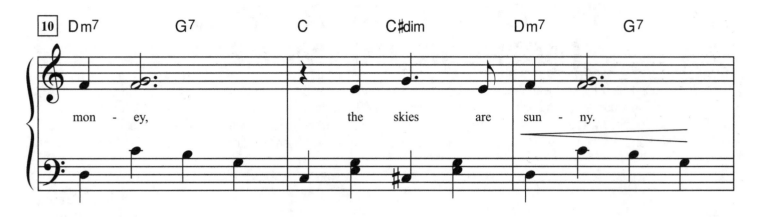

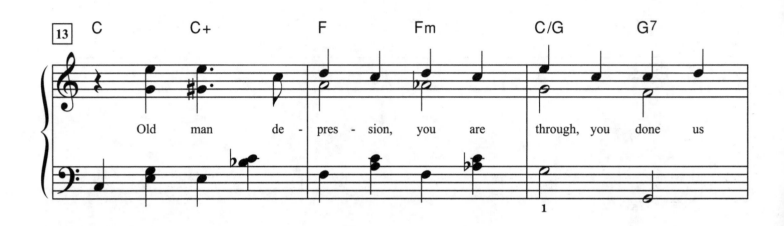

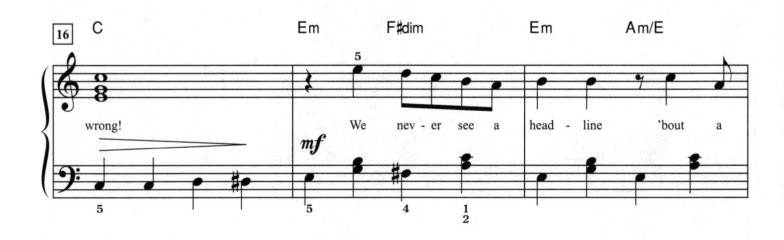

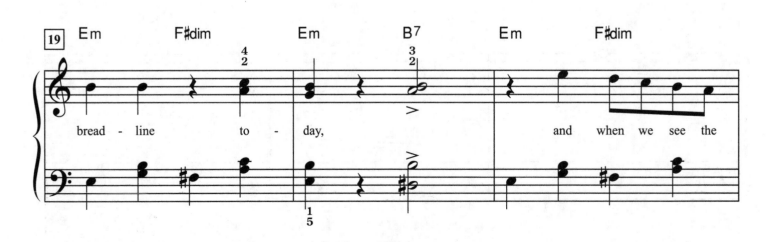

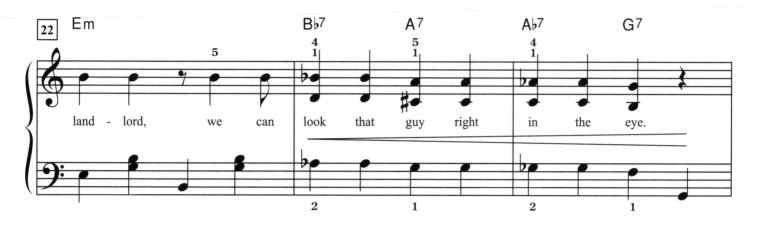

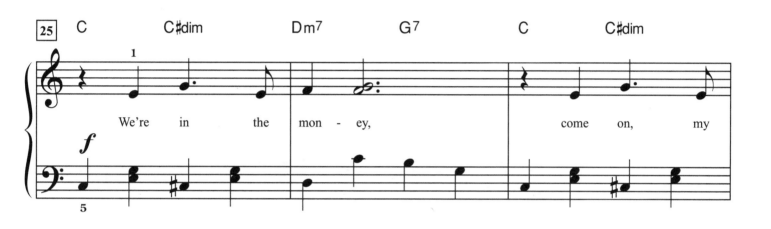

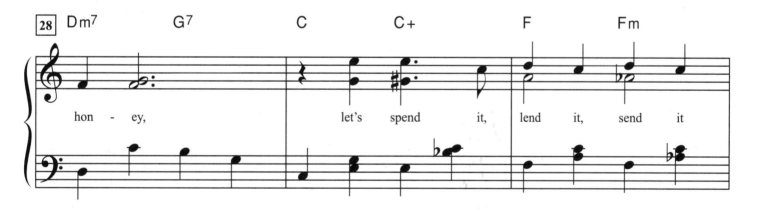

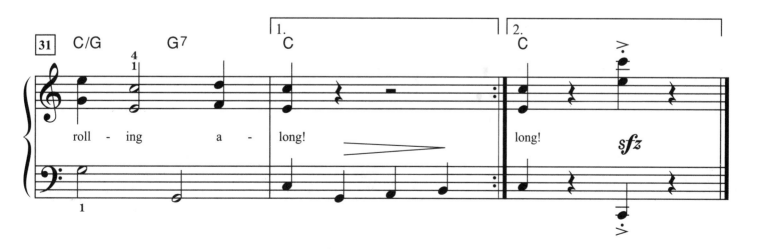

GOOD MORNING

The 1939 hit movie *Babes in Arms*, starring Mickey Rooney and Judy Garland, was based on the 1937 Rodgers and Hart musical of the same name. "Good Morning" was written for the movie and later was featured in the 1952 classic film *Singin' in the Rain*.

Words by Arthur Freed
Music by Nacio Herb Brown
Arranged by Dan Coates

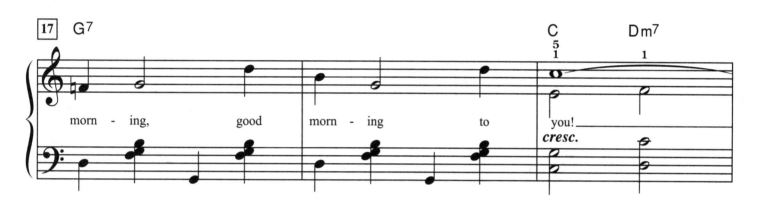

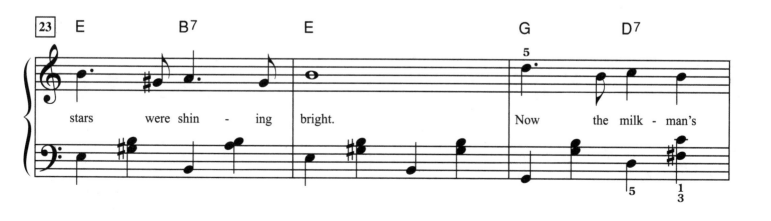

50

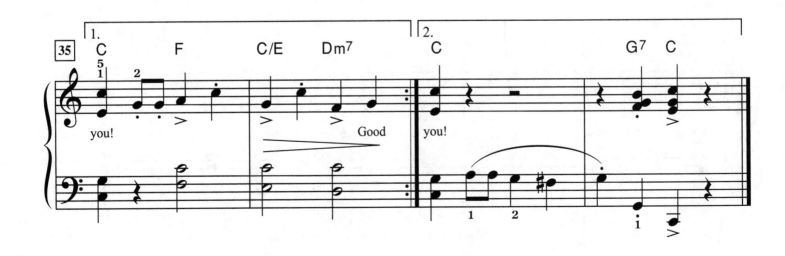

HOORAY FOR HOLLYWOOD

"Hooray for Hollywood" has become the melody most associated with movie award nights and Hollywood in general. It was first used in the 1937 film *Hollywood Hotel,* which starred 26-year-old Ronald Reagan, who was building an acting career at the time. He was elected as president of the Screen Actors Guild in 1947 and, of course, eventually became President of the United States. Hooray for Hollywood, indeed.

Words by Johnny Mercer
Music by Richard A. Whiting
Arranged by Dan Coates

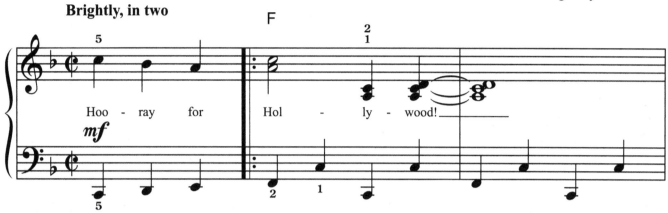

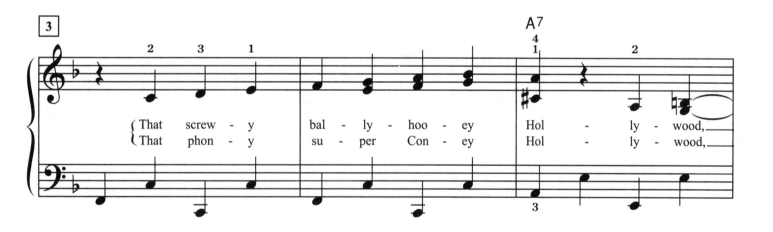

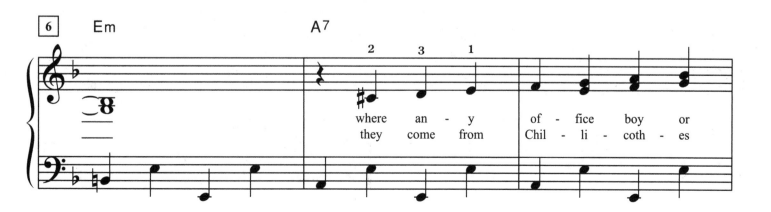

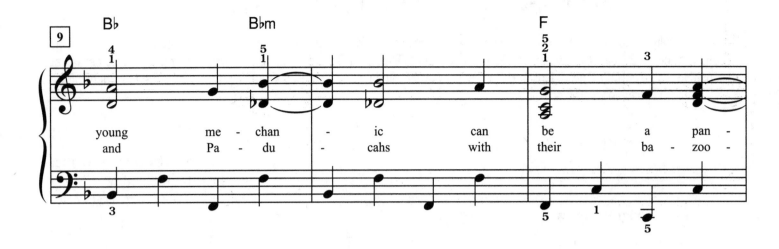

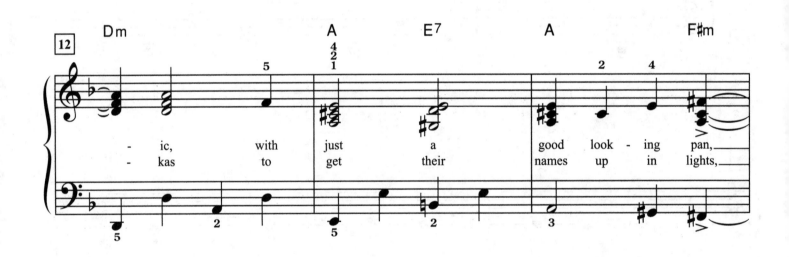

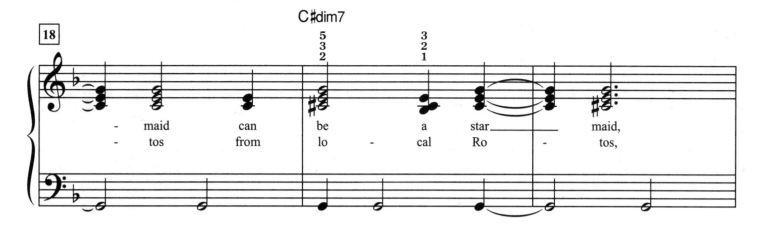

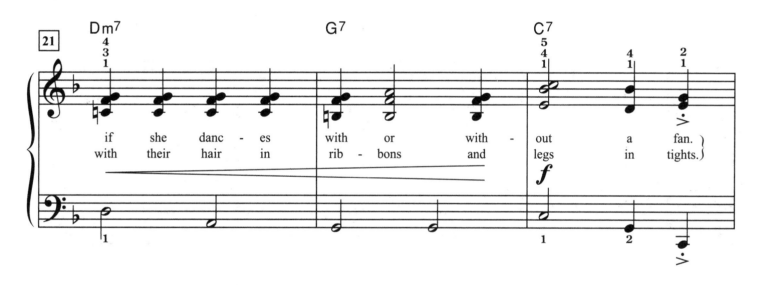

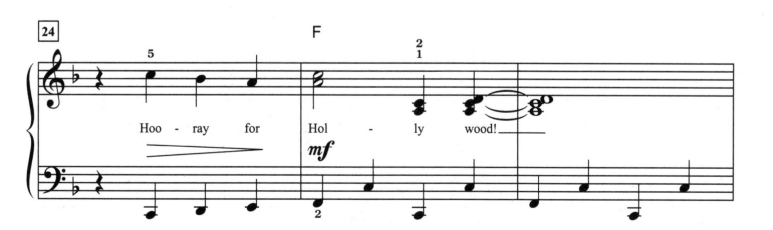

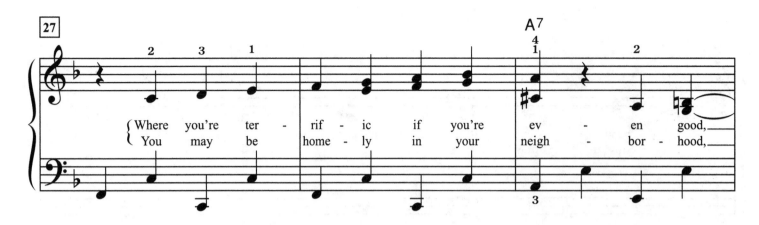

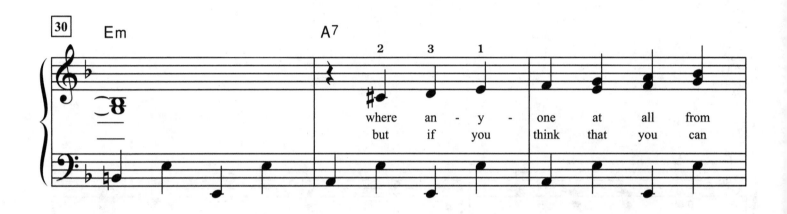

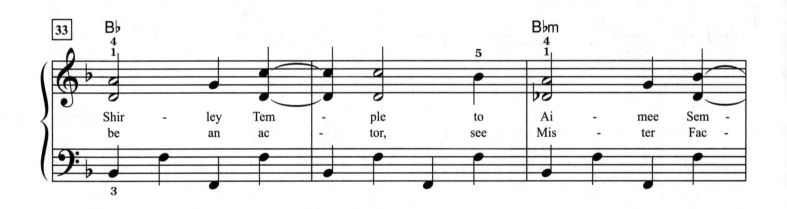

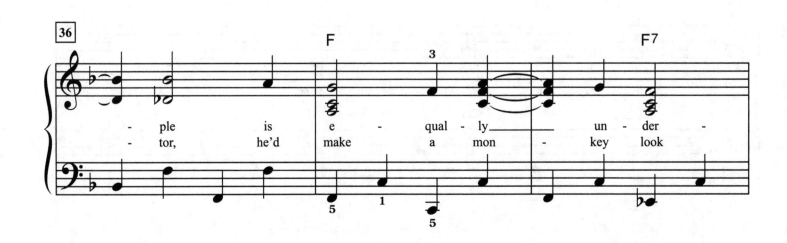

GOODY GOODY

"Goody Goody" was first popularized by a recording made by Helen Ward—one of the first female swing singers—and the Benny Goodman Orchestra. Years later, 1950s pop idol Frankie Lymon had a hit with his solo version.

Words by Johnny Mercer
Music by Matt Malneck
Arranged by Dan Coates

So you met some-one who set___ you back on your

heels, good-y good-y! So you met some-one and now___

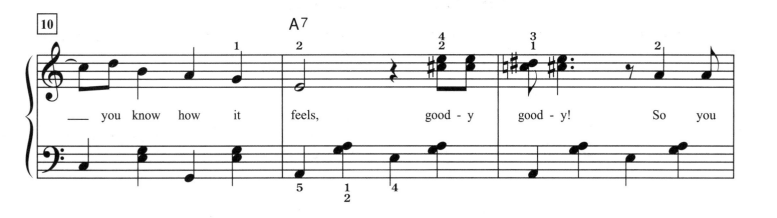

you know how it feels, good - y good - y! So you

gave him your heart too just like I gave mine to

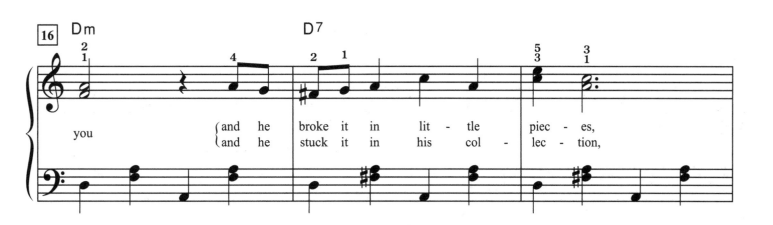

you {and he broke it in lit - tle piec - es,
{and he stuck it in his col - lec - tion,

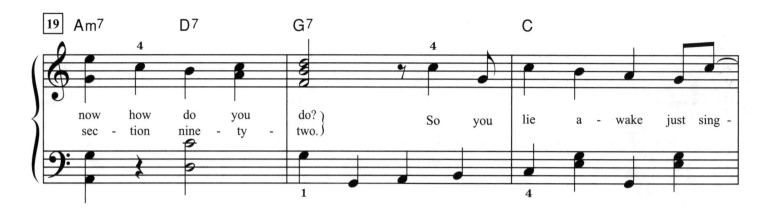

now how do you do?
sec - tion nine - ty - two. } So you lie a - wake just sing -

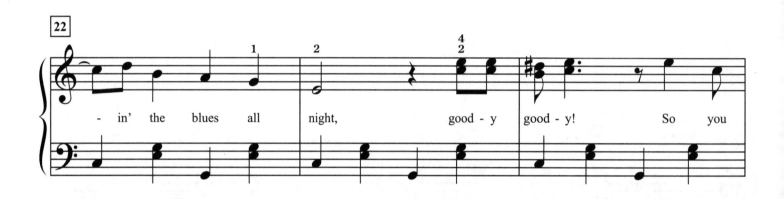

- in' the blues all night, good - y good - y! So you

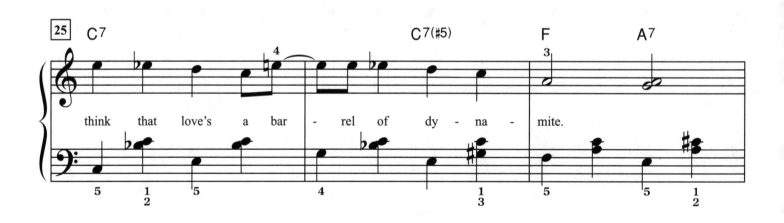

think that love's a bar - rel of dy - na - mite.

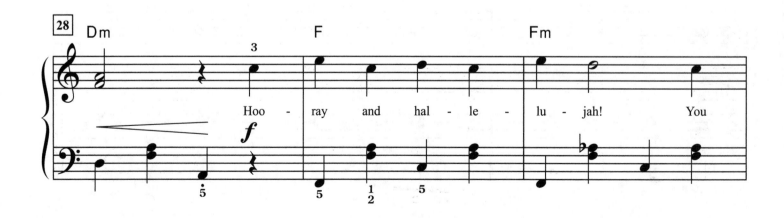

Hoo - ray and hal - le - lu - jah! You

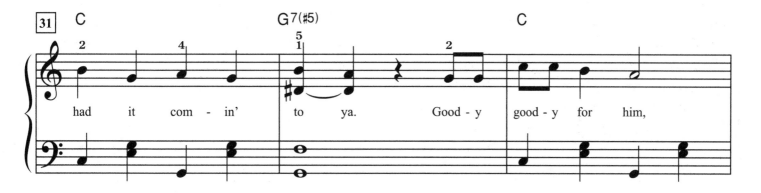

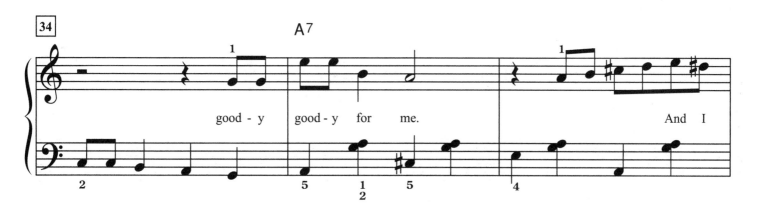

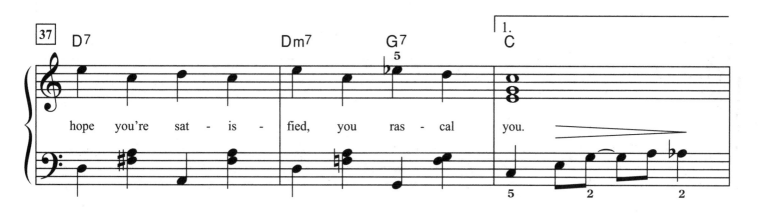

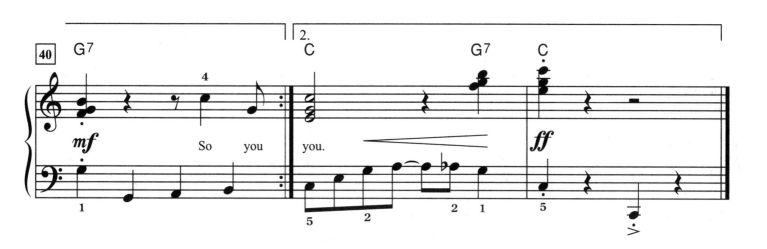

I GET A KICK OUT OF YOU

One of the hits from the musical *Anything Goes,* "I Get a Kick Out of You" was originally sung by Ethel Merman. Many other singers—from Frank Sinatra to Patti Lupone—have performed this song, often varying the lyrics. "I Get a Kick Out of You," through all of its variations, remains a lighthearted expression of affection in the Broadway style.

Words and Music by Cole Porter
Arranged by Dan Coates

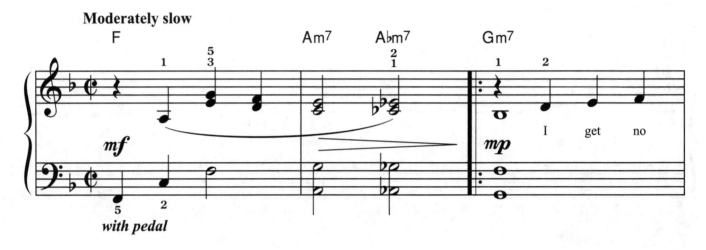

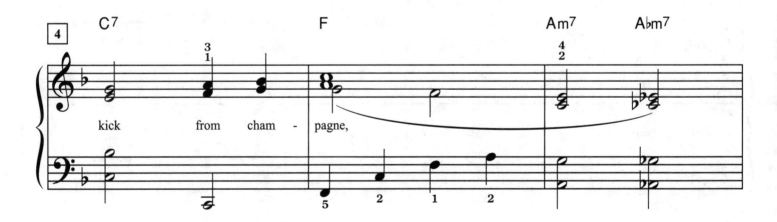

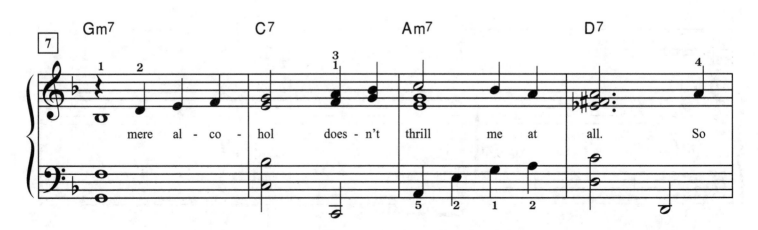

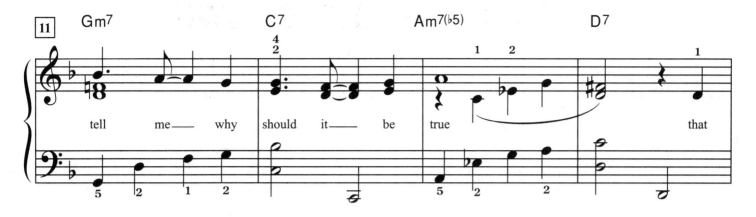

tell me—— why should it—— be true that

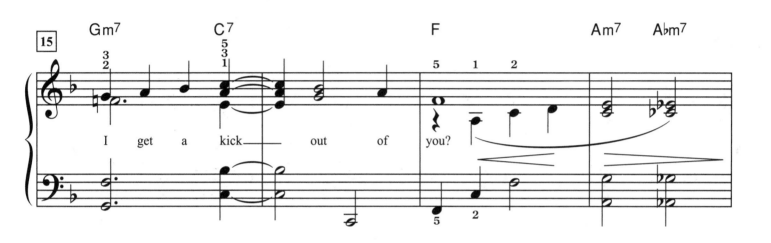

I get a kick—— out of you?

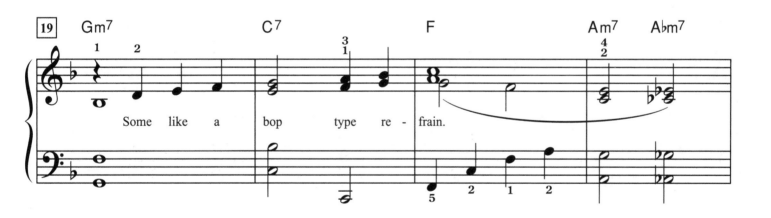

Some like a bop type re - frain.

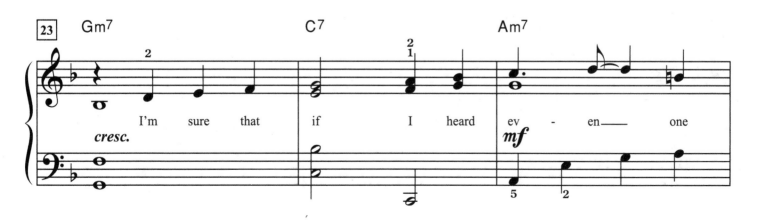

I'm sure that if I heard ev - en—— one

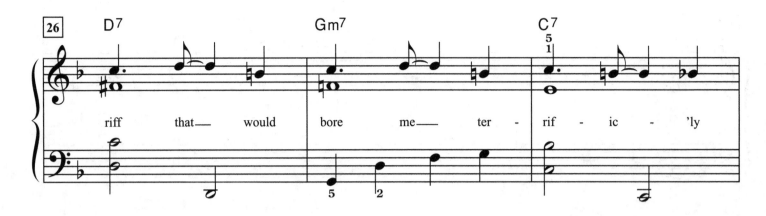

riff that would bore me terrific'ly

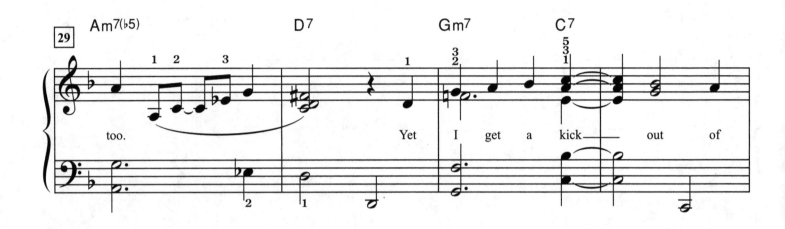

too. Yet I get a kick out of

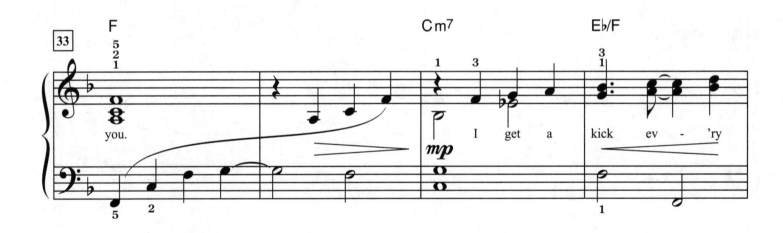

you. I get a kick ev'ry

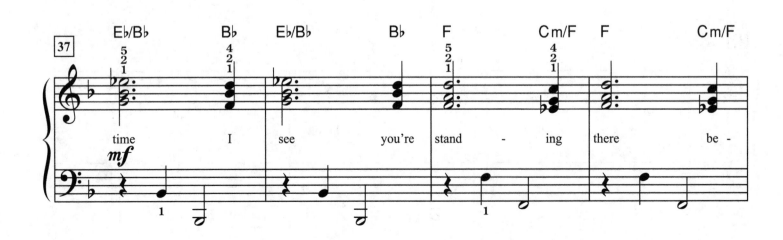

time I see you're stand - ing there be -

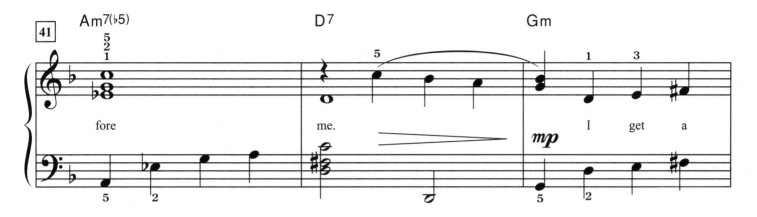

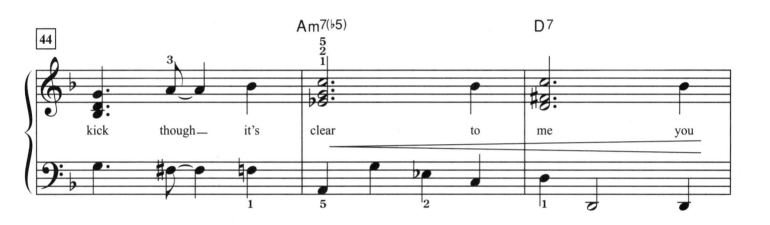

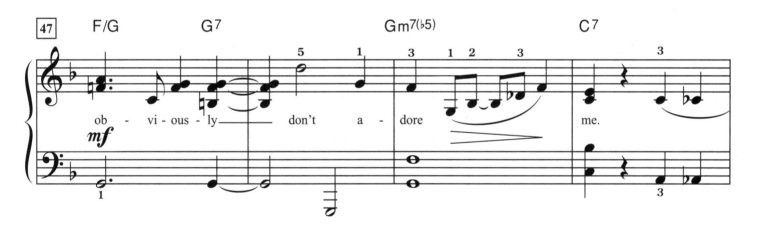

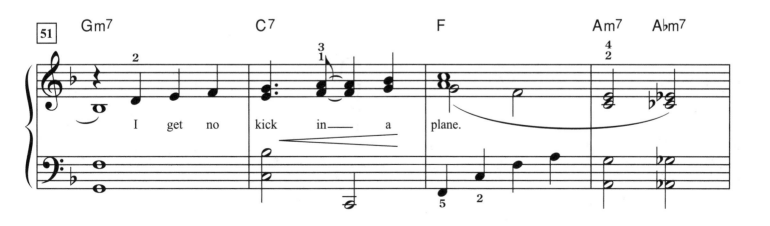

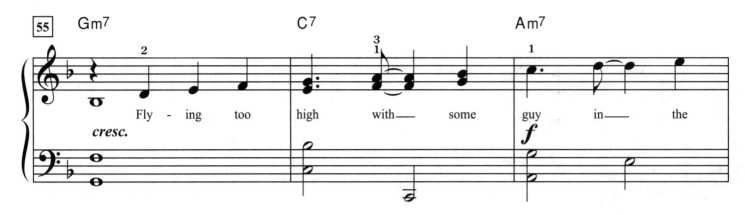

Fly - ing too high with— some guy in— the

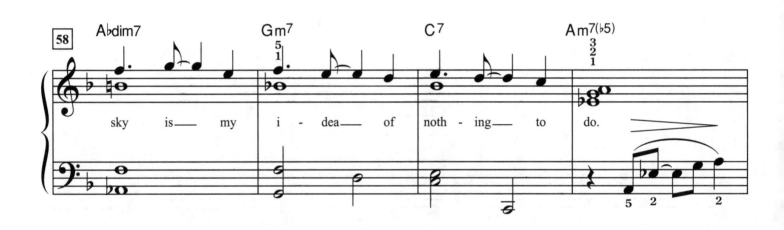

sky is— my i - dea— of noth - ing— to do.

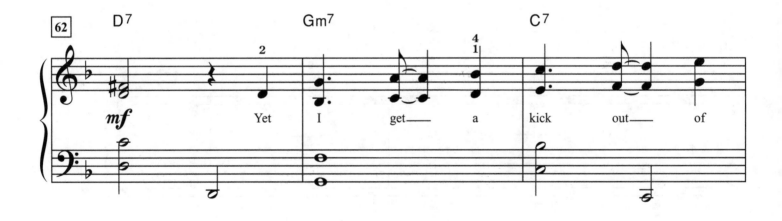

Yet I get— a kick out— of

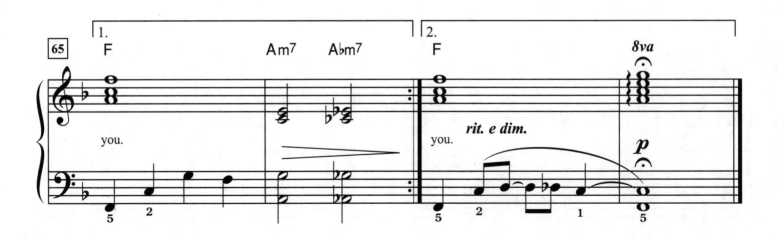

you.

you.

I GOT RHYTHM

Like so many jazz standards, "I Got Rhythm" originated in a musical. George and Ira Gershwin's *Girl Crazy* (1930) made stars of Ethel Merman and Judy Garland, and also introduced the world to many Gershwin classics including "But Not for Me" (page 28), "Embraceable You" (page 37), and "I Got Rhythm." In 1933, George Gershwin expanded "I Got Rhythm" into *Variations on "I Got Rhythm"* for piano and orchestra, which became his final classical concert piece. It was the only work he dedicated to his brother Ira.

Music and Lyrics by
George Gershwin and Ira Gershwin
Arranged by Dan Coates

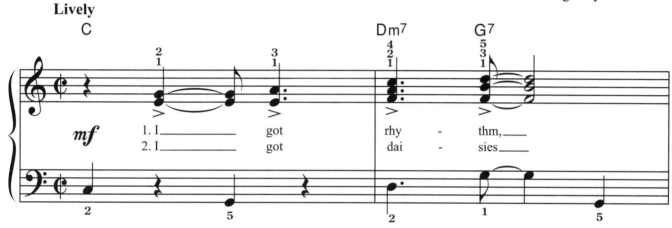

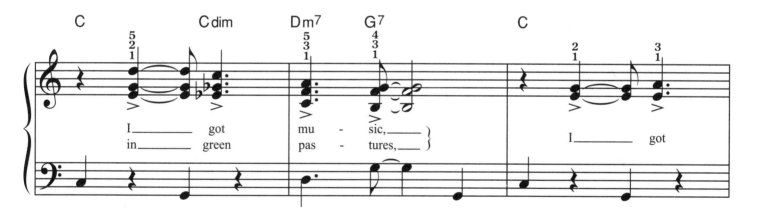

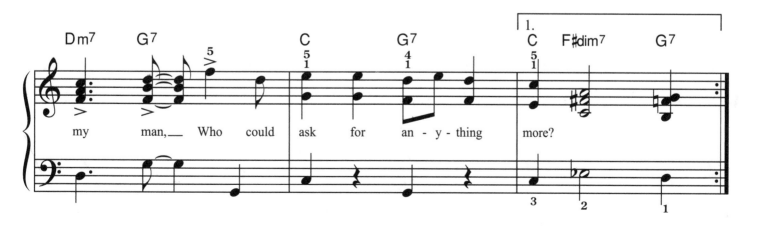

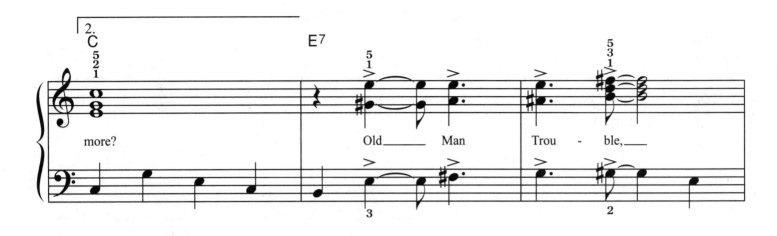

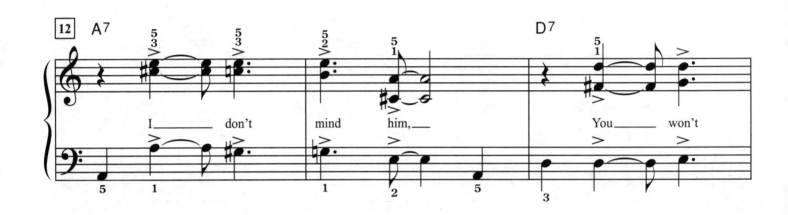

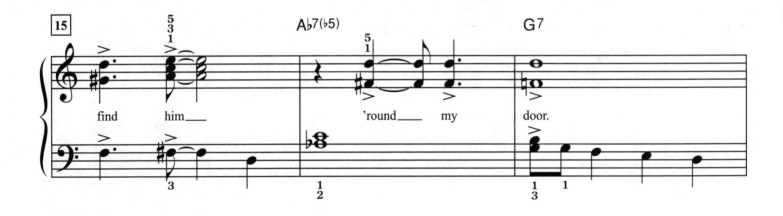

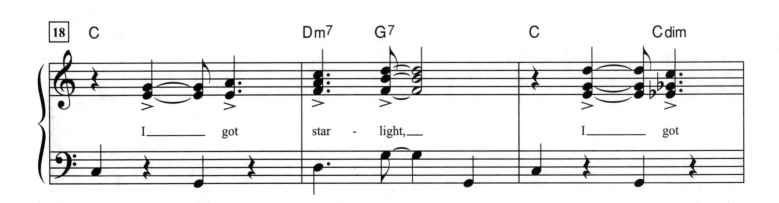

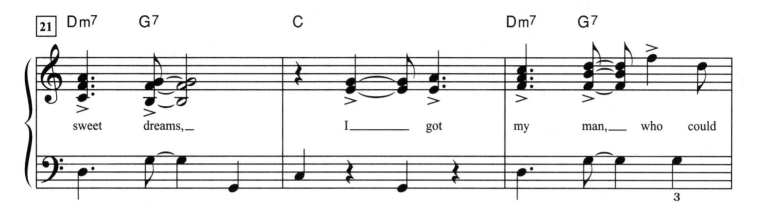

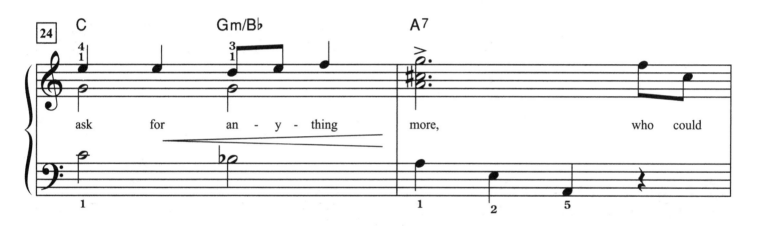

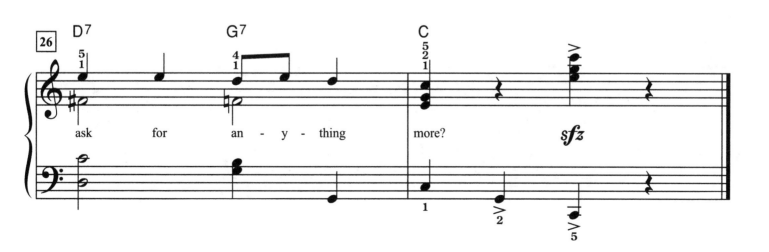

I ONLY HAVE EYES FOR YOU

"I Only Have Eyes for You" is not only known as a standard but also as a 1950s pop song, made famous by The Flamingos. It was originally written for the 1934 musical film *Dames,* and in 1989 it won an ASCAP award for Most Performed Feature Film Standard. Many notable artists have recorded the song including Frank Sinatra, Peggy Lee and Art Garfunkel.

Words by Al Dubin
Music by Harry Warren
Arranged by Dan Coates

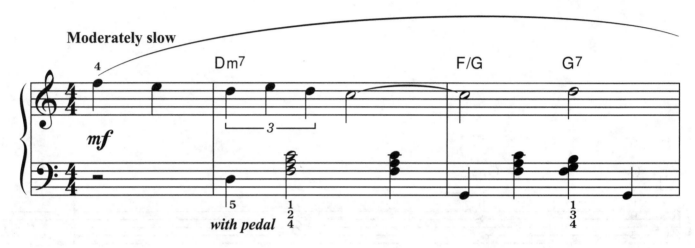

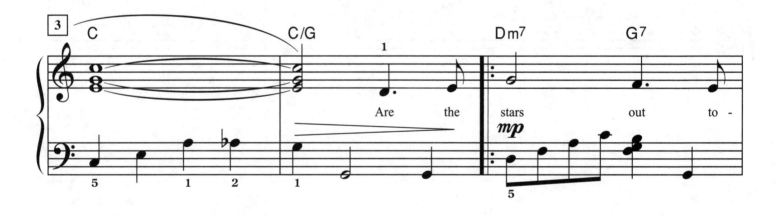

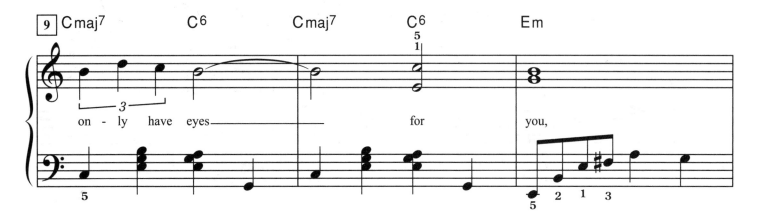

on - ly have eyes _____ for you,

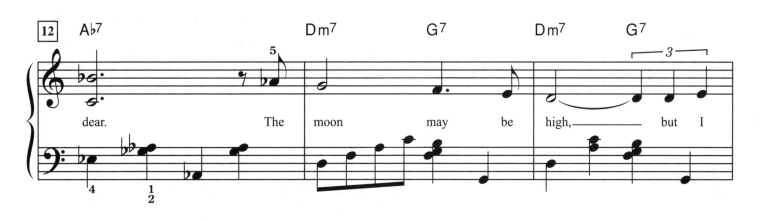

dear. The moon may be high, _____ but I

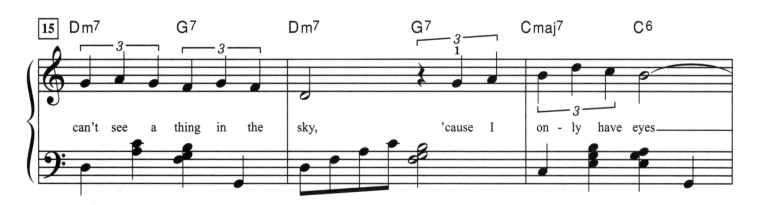

can't see a thing in the sky, 'cause I on - ly have eyes _____

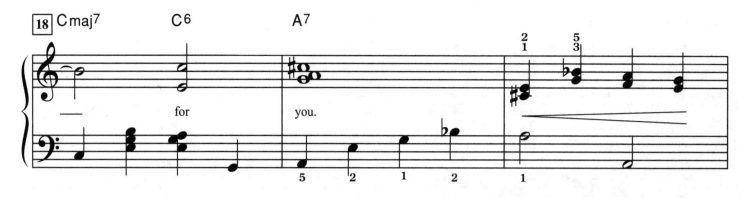

for you.

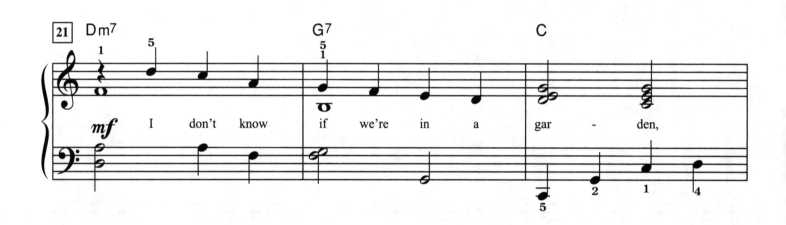

I don't know if we're in a gar - den,

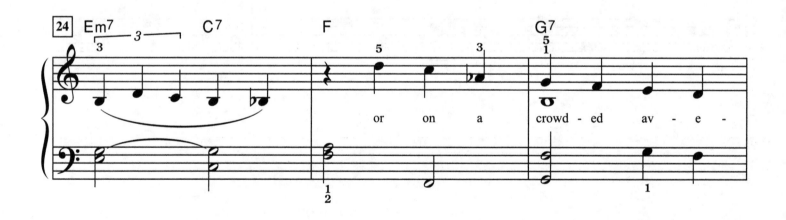

or on a crowd - ed av - e -

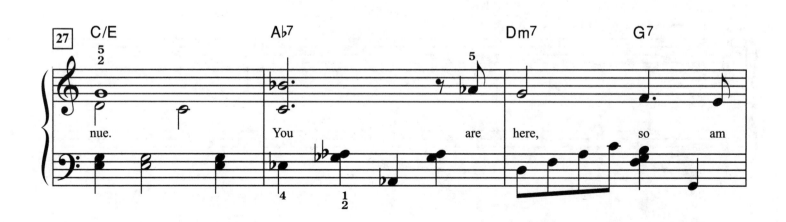

nue. You are here, so am

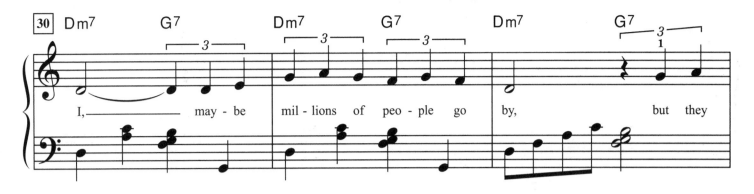

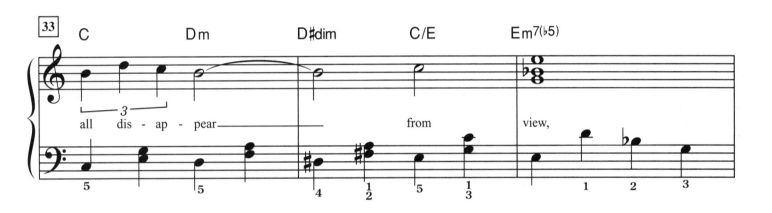

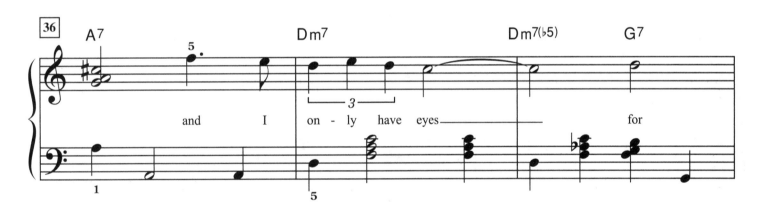

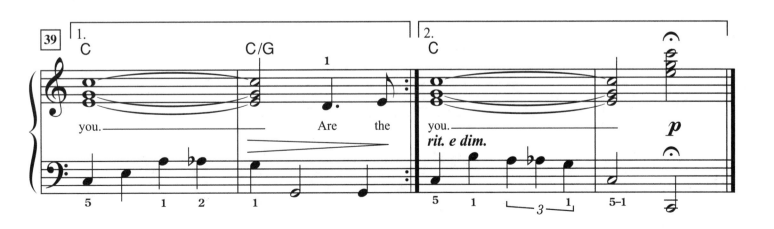

I'LL BE SEEING YOU

"I'll Be Seeing You" is from the obscure 1938 musical *Right This Way*. (It ran for just 15 performances.) The song's beautiful melody was written by Sammy Fain ("Are You Havin' Any Fun," page 7). The tune became a classic during World War II when many were separated from the ones they loved. In the 1950s, prime-time piano celebrity Liberace used "I'll Be Seeing You" as the theme to his popular television program *The Liberace Show*.

Lyrics by Irving Kahal
Music by Sammy Fain
Arranged by Dan Coates

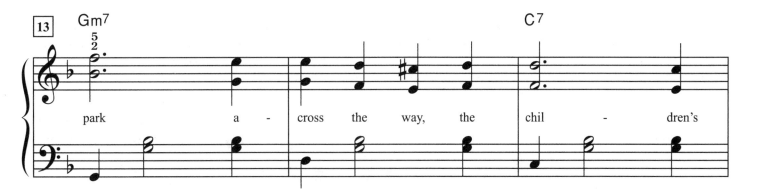

park a - cross the way, the chil - dren's

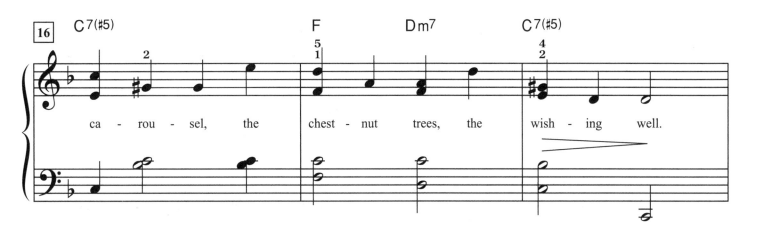

ca - rou - sel, the chest - nut trees, the wish - ing well.

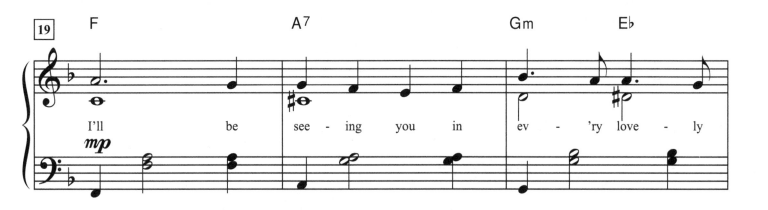

I'll be see - ing you in ev - 'ry love - ly

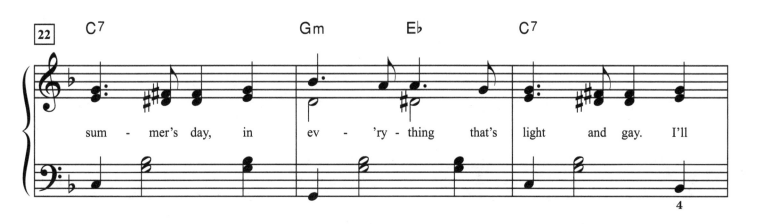

sum - mer's day, in ev - 'ry - thing that's light and gay. I'll

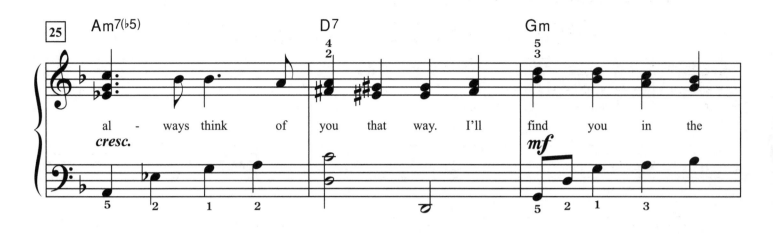

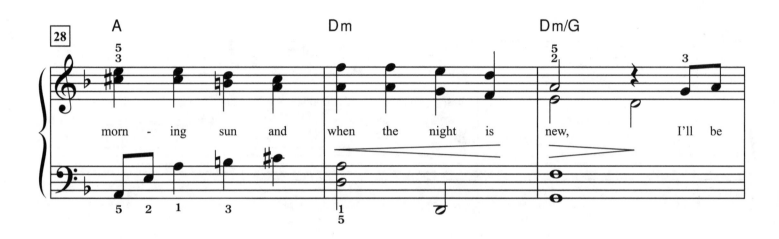

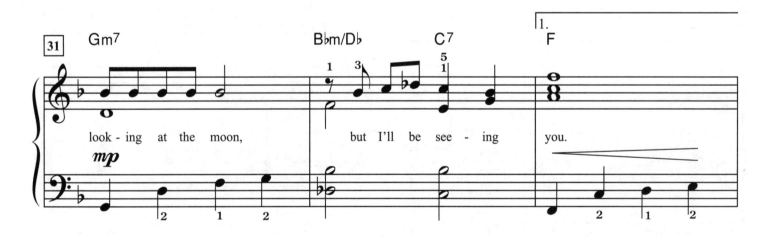

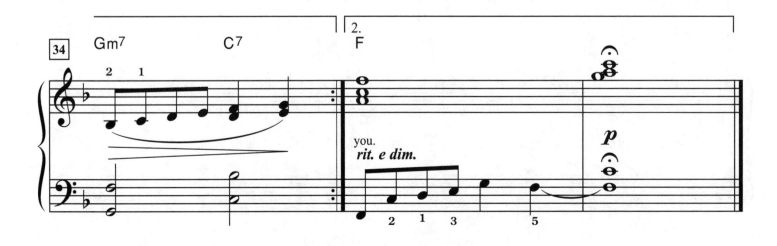

I'M GONNA SIT RIGHT DOWN AND WRITE MYSELF A LETTER

"I'm Gonna Sit Right Down and Write Myself a Letter" was made famous by jazz pianist Fats Waller's 1935 recording. Waller is best known for his "stride" style of piano playing, his energetic performances in the United States and Europe, and his Grammy Hall of Fame-inducted recordings of "Ain't Misbehavin'" and "Honeysuckle Rose."

Words by Joe Young
Music by Fred E. Ahlert
Arranged by Dan Coates

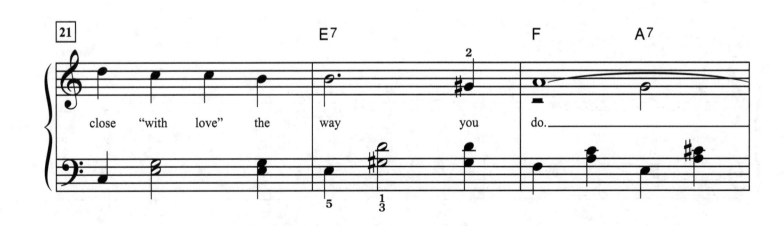

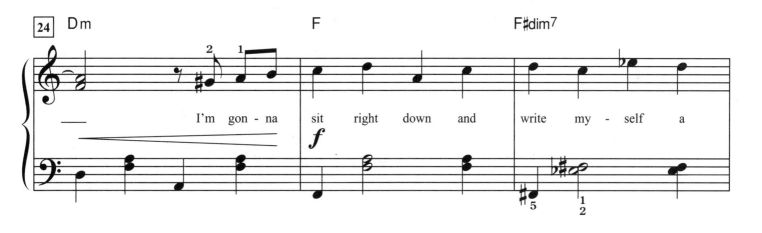

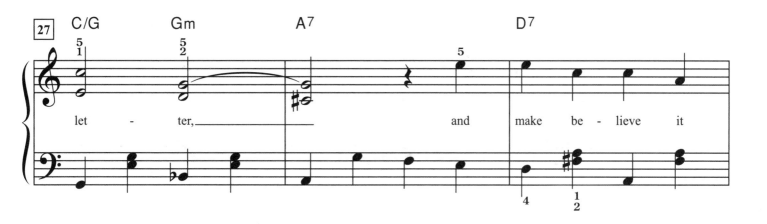

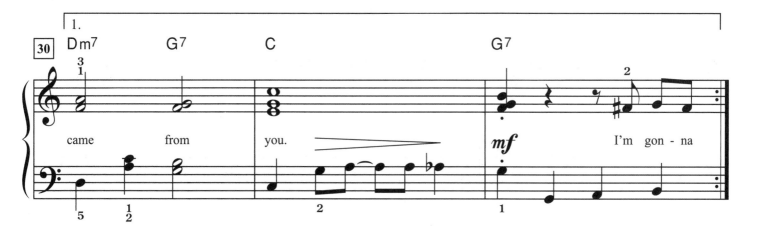

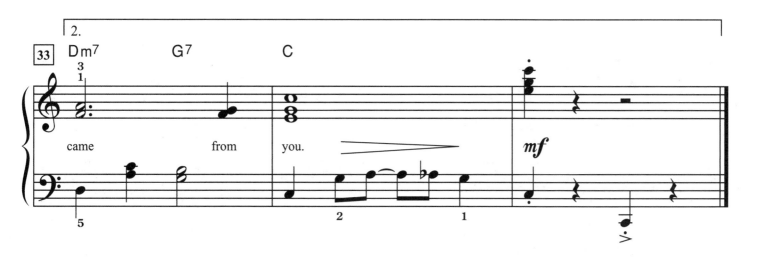

I'M IN THE MOOD FOR LOVE

"I'm in the Mood for Love" was first sung by Frances Langford in her film debut, *Every Night at Eight* (1935). She would star in many other films and would also perform regularly on U.S.O. tours during World War II. "I'm in the Mood for Love" became her signature song. Years later, it would also become the signature song for the character Alfalfa on the popular television series *Our Gang* (a.k.a. *The Little Rascals*).

Words and Music by
Jimmy McHugh and Dorothy Fields
Arranged by Dan Coates

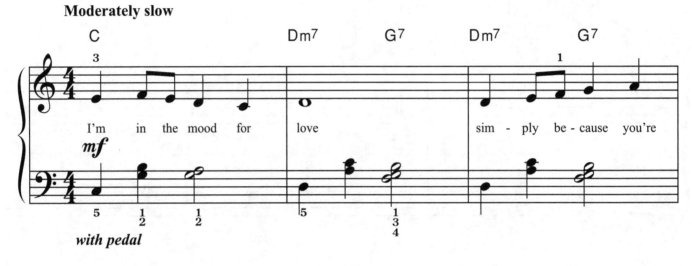

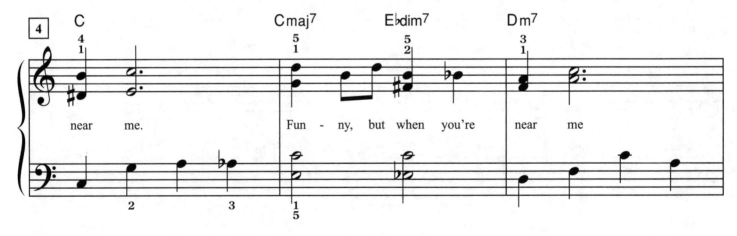

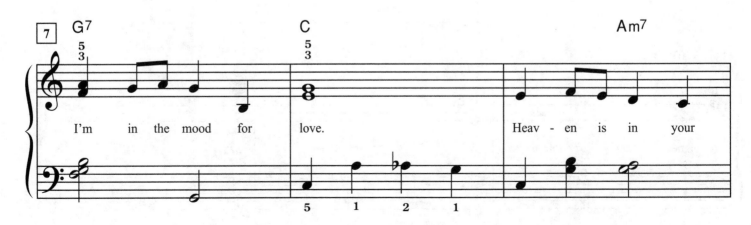

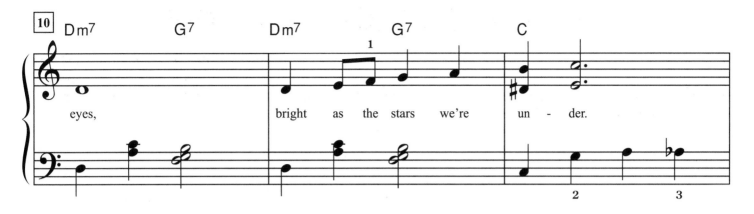

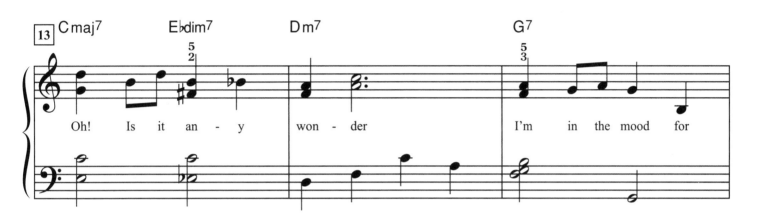

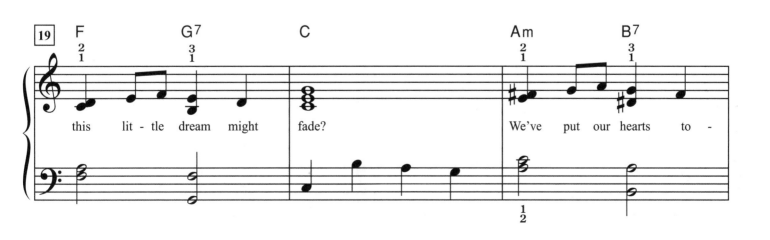

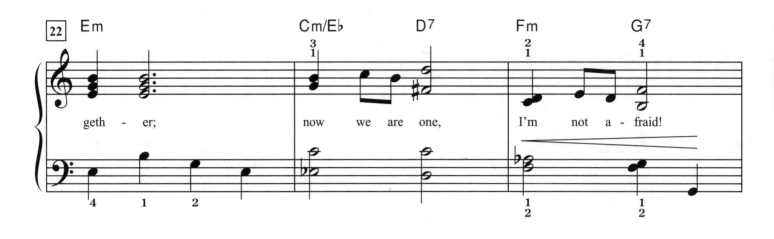

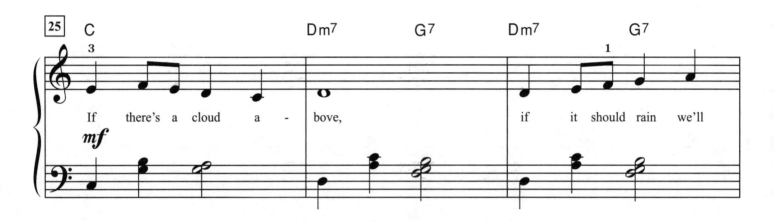

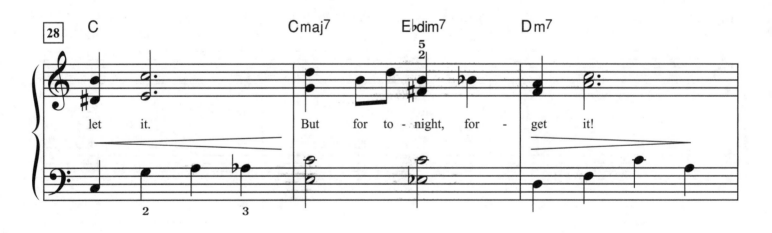

IN THE STILL OF THE NIGHT

"In the Still of the Night" was first used in the 1937 musical film *Rosalie*, a story of a princess from a faraway land who falls in love with a West Point military cadet. The film featured the tap dancing talents of Eleanor Powell and new music composed by Cole Porter. Unlike many of the great songwriters of the era, Porter wrote both the music and lyrics for his compositions.

Words and Music by Cole Porter
Arranged by Dan Coates

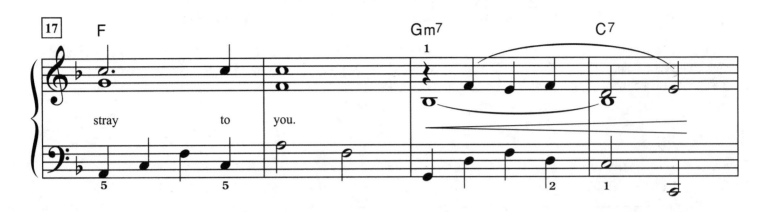

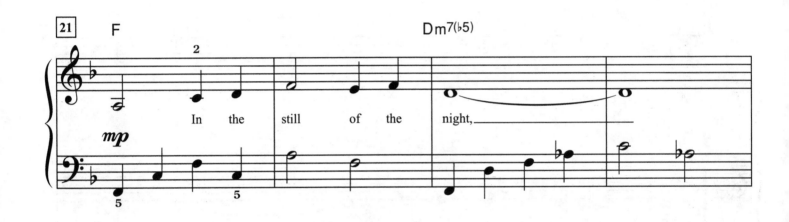

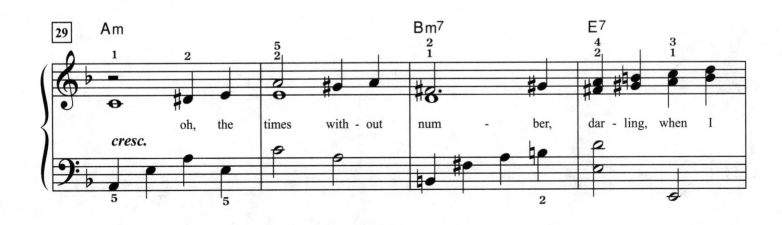

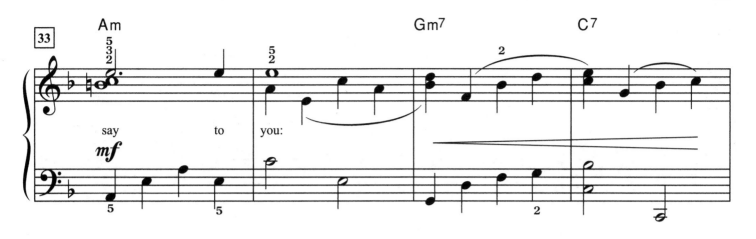

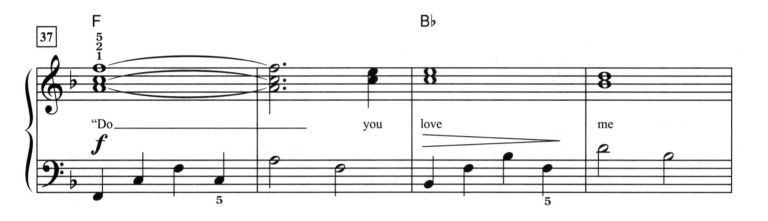

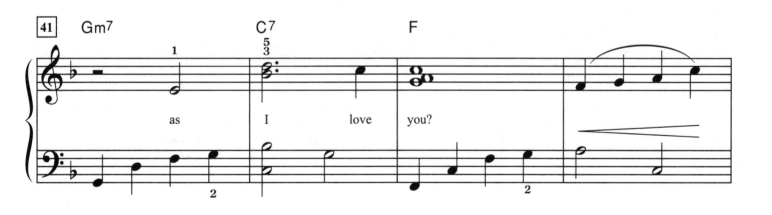

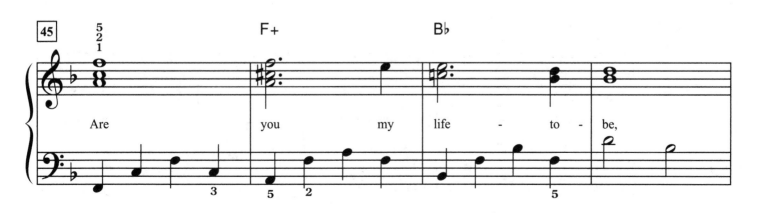

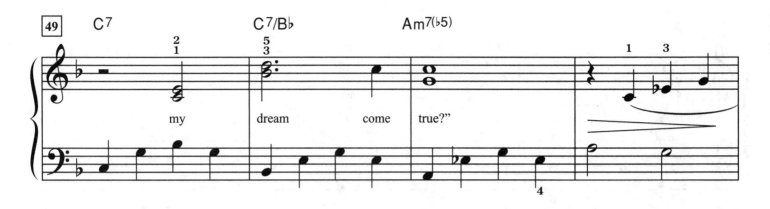

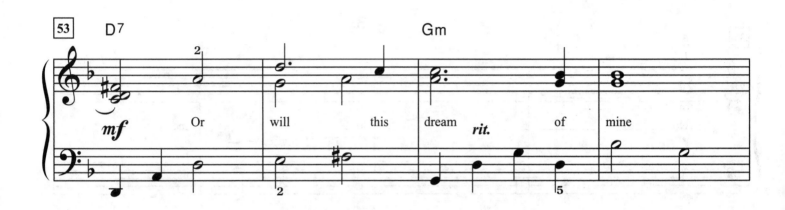

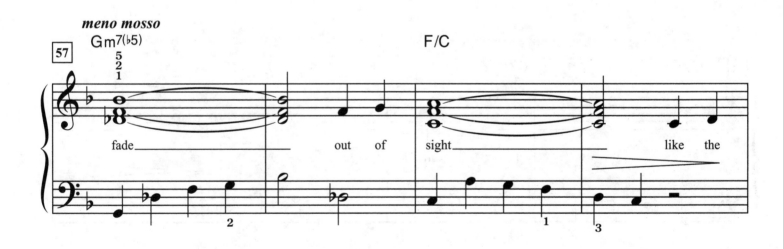

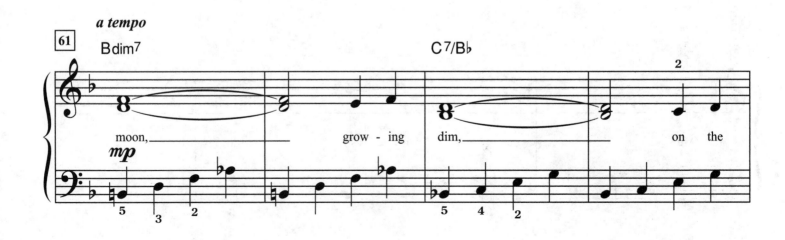

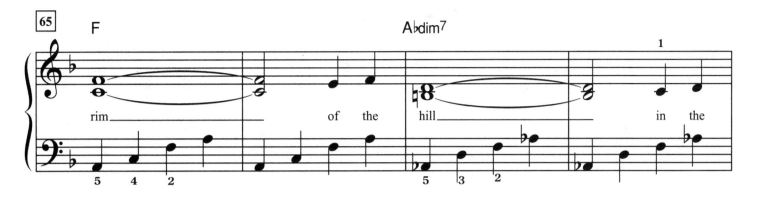

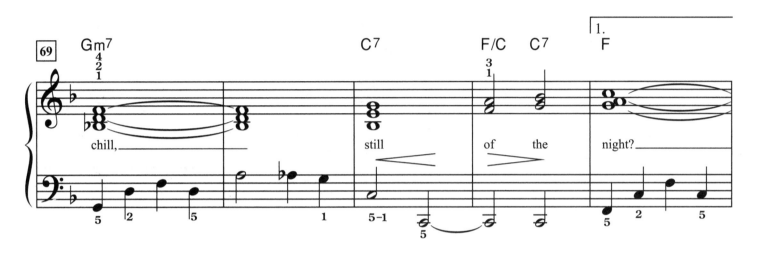

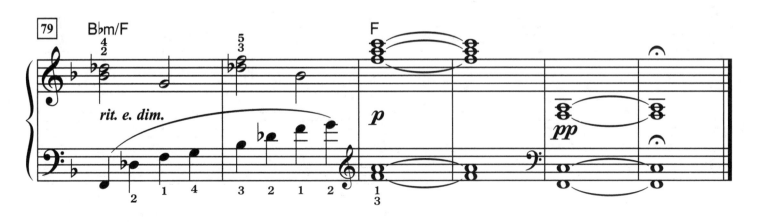

IT'S DE-LOVELY

"It's De-Lovely" is from the popular 1936 musical *Red Hot and Blue,* which starred the all-star trio of Ethel Merman, Jimmy Durante and Bob Hope. The song was later used in the 1962 revival of *Anything Goes* and was also the name of the 2004 biographical film about Cole Porter, *De-Lovely.*

Words and Music by Cole Porter
Arranged by Dan Coates

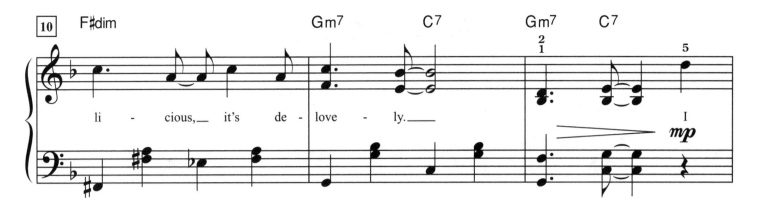

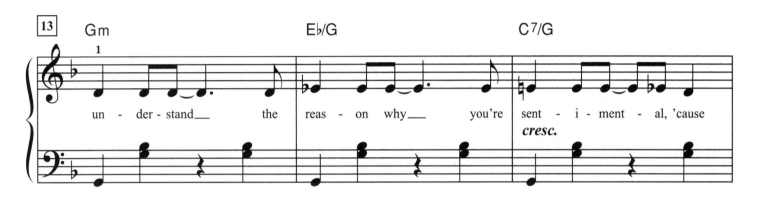

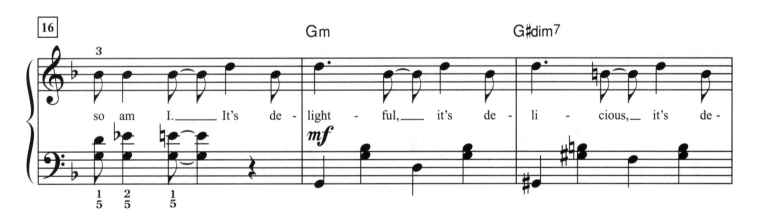

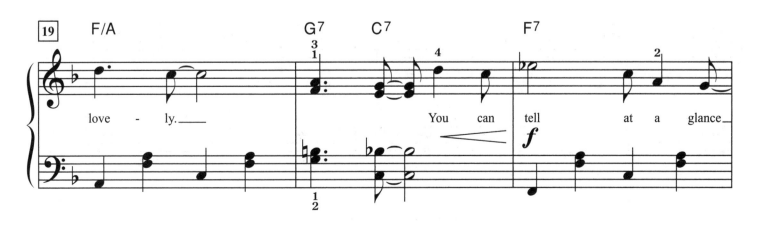

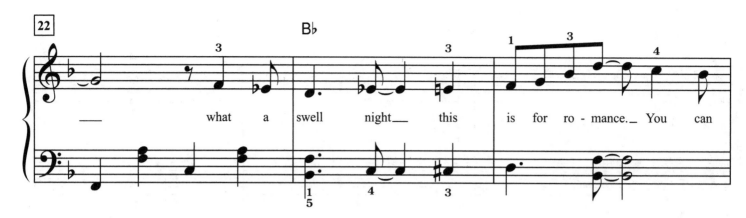

what a swell night___ this is for ro - mance.___ You can

hear dear Moth - er Na - ture mur - mur - ing low, "Let

your-self go."___ So please be sweet,___ my chick - a - dee,___ and

when I kiss___ you, just say to me,___ "It's de - light - ful,___ it's de -

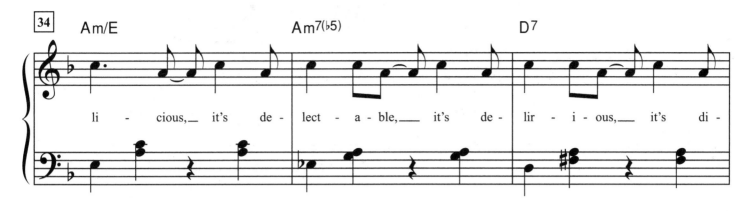

li - cious,___ it's de - lect - a - ble,___ it's de - lir - i - ous,___ it's di -

lem - ma it's___ de - li - mit, it's de - luxe, it's de - love - ly."___

The

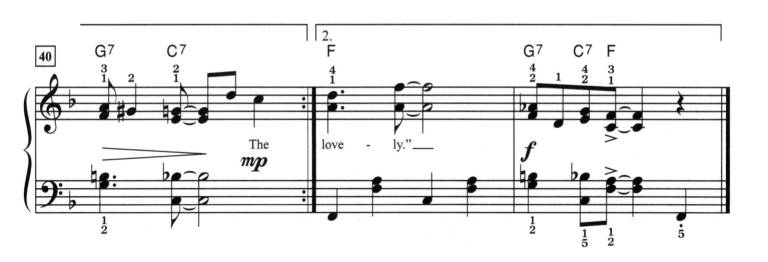

love - ly."___

IT'S ONLY A PAPER MOON

Harold Arlen, E. Y. Harburg and Billy Rose wrote "It's Only a Paper Moon" in 1933, and it has since become a standard for jazz singers and musicians. Billy Rose requested a cynical love song for his Broadway production *The Great Magoo*. It was the only song used in the show, reprised frequently throughout the production by leading lady Sandy Faison. Although critics enjoyed Faison's lilting voice, *The Great Magoo* flopped. However, decades later countless artists would have hits with their renditions of "It's Only a Paper Moon" including Nat King Cole, Tony Bennett, Dave Brubeck, Bing Crosby, Marvin Gaye and Ella Fitzgerald.

Words by Billy Rose and E.Y. Harburg
Music by Harold Arlen
Arranged by Dan Coates

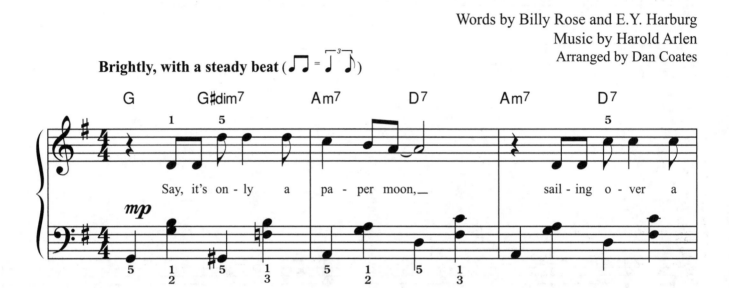

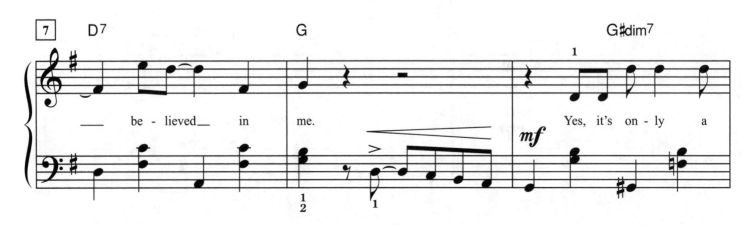

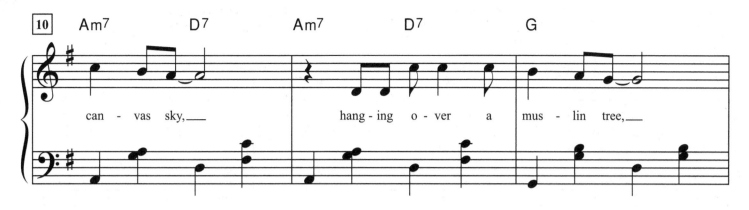

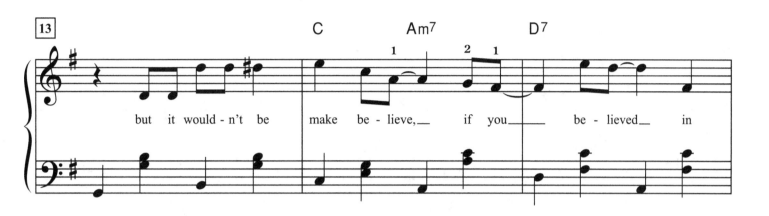

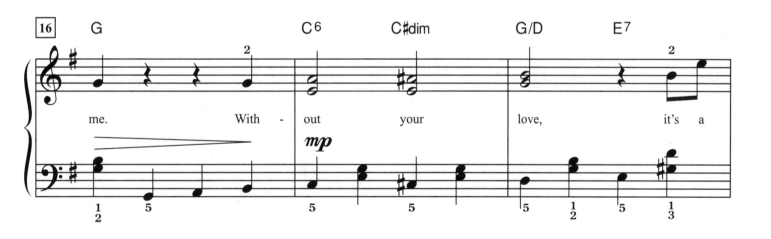

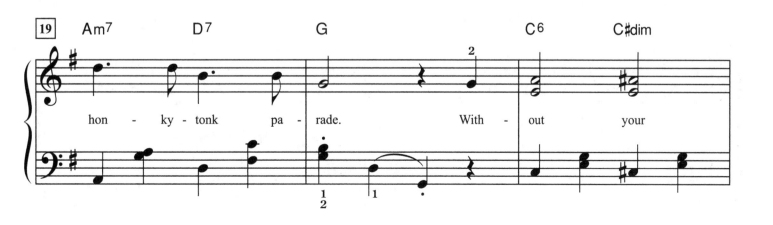

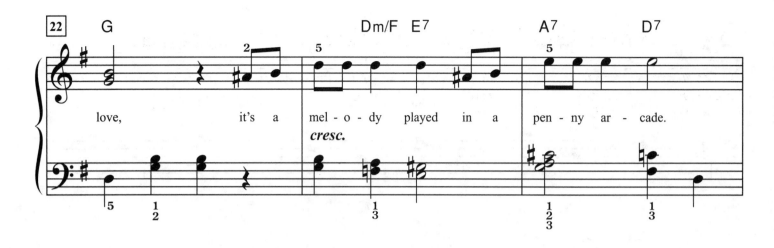

22 G — Dm/F E7 — A7 — D7

love, it's a mel-o-dy played in a pen-ny ar-cade.

cresc.

25 G — G#dim7 — Am7 — D7 — Am7 — D7

mf

It's a Bar-num and Bai-ley world,___ just as phon-y as

28 G — C — Am7

it can be,___ but it would-n't be make be-lieve___ if you___

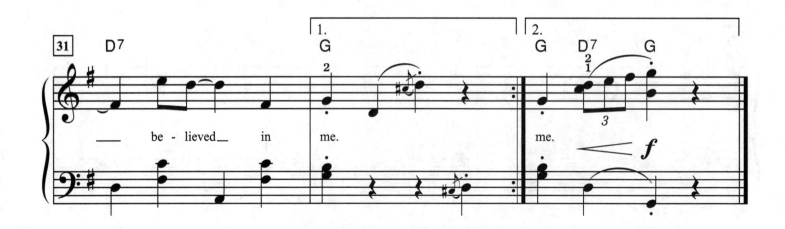

31 D7 — 1. G — 2. G D7 G

___ be-lieved___ in me. me.

f

I'VE GOT YOU UNDER MY SKIN

"I've Got You Under My Skin" was written in 1936 and first performed by Virginia Bruce in the MGM musical film *Born to Dance*. It was nominated for the Academy Award for Best Song in 1936 and would later become a signature song for Frank Sinatra as well as a Top 10 recording for the Four Seasons.

Words and Music by Cole Porter
Arranged by Dan Coates

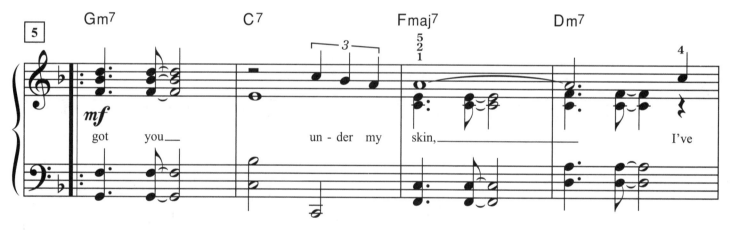

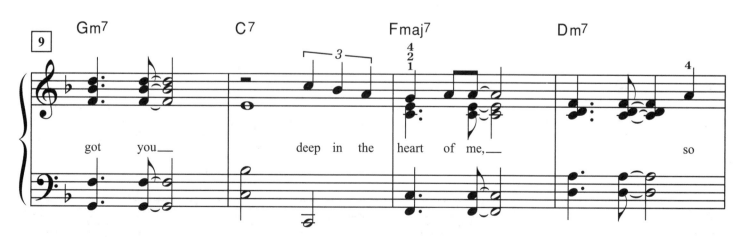

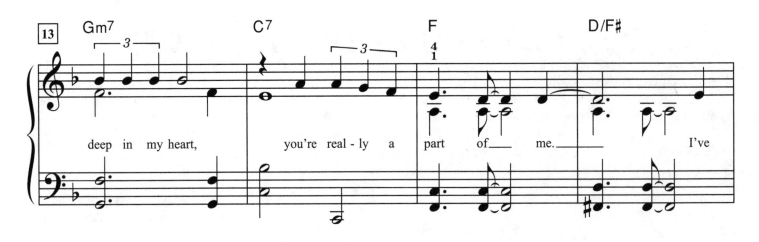

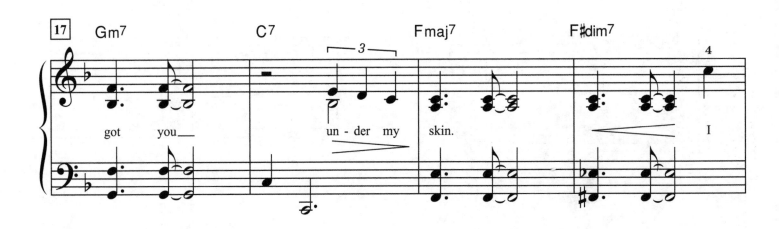

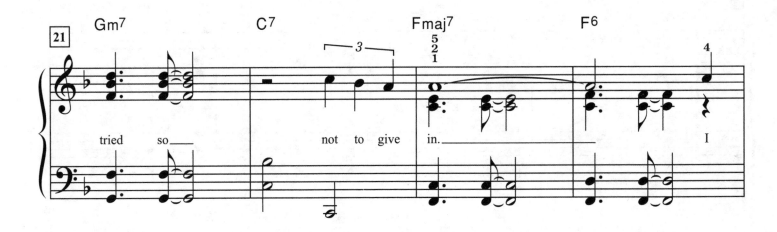

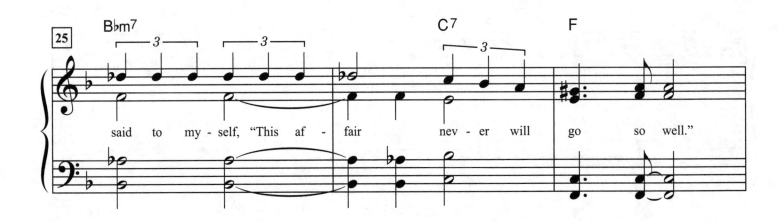

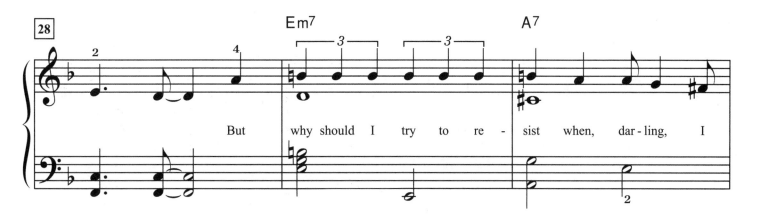

But why should I try to re- sist when, dar - ling, I

know so well I've got you

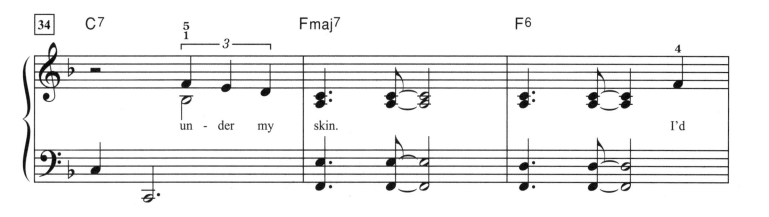

un - der my skin. I'd

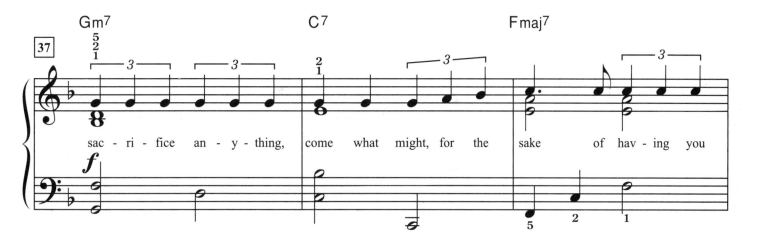

sac - ri - fice an - y - thing, come what might, for the sake of hav - ing you

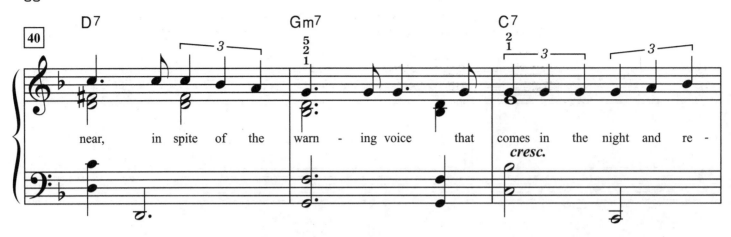

near, in spite of the warn - ing voice that comes in the night and re-
cresc.

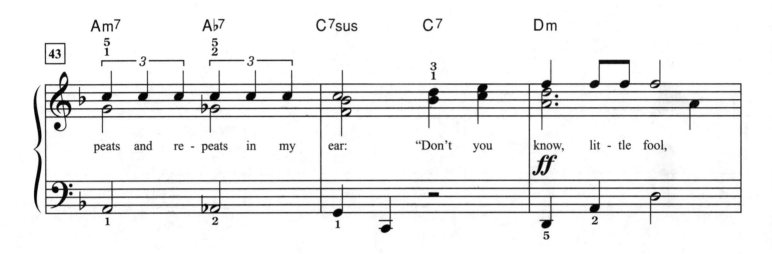

peats and re - peats in my ear: "Don't you know, lit - tle fool,
ff

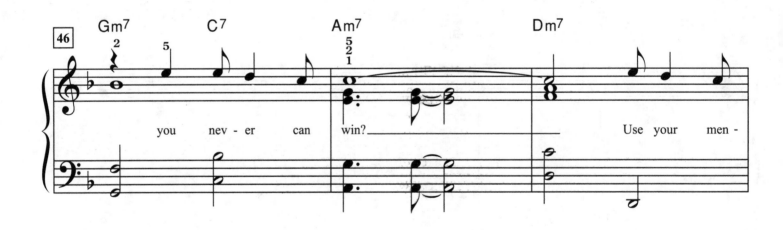

you nev - er can win?_____ Use your men-

tal - i - ty, wake up to re - al - i - ty."

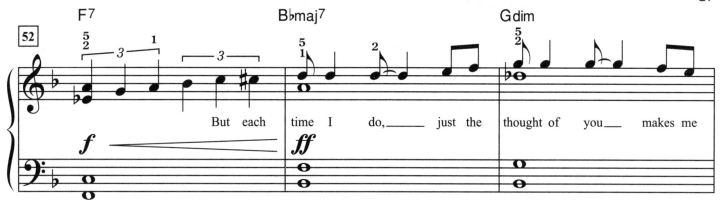

But each time I do,_____ just the thought of you___ makes me

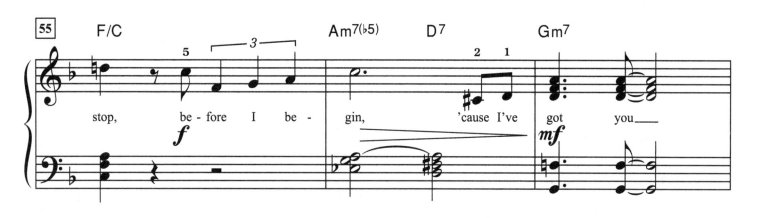

stop, be - fore I be - gin, 'cause I've got you___

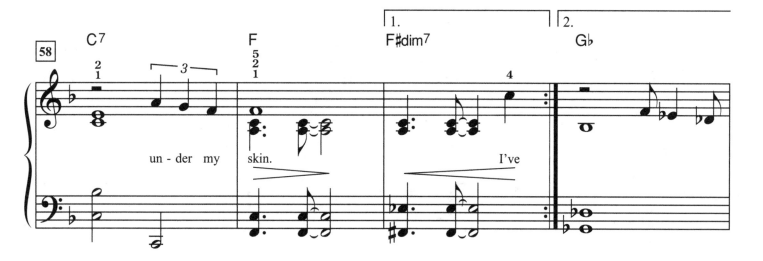

un - der my skin. I've

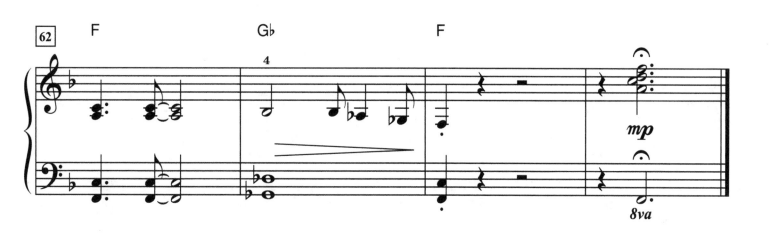

JEEPERS CREEPERS

In the 1938 comedic film *Going Places*, Louis Armstrong plays a race horse trainer. In order to calm Jeepers Creepers, a very wild race horse, Armstrong plays his trumpet for the unruly animal. This is the only method that will work. The stallion's favorite song is, of course, "Jeepers Creepers," which his trainer has written for him. The song begins: *Jeepers Creepers! Where'd ya get those peepers? Jeepers Creepers! Where'd ya get those eyes?*

Words by Johnny Mercer
Music by Harry Warren
Arranged by Dan Coates

JUST ONE OF THOSE THINGS

"Just One of Those Things" is from the 1935 musical *Jubilee* about a royal family in a fictitious European country who leave their responsibilities to pursue relationships with commoners. The King involves himself with a party hostess; the Queen falls for a hunky movie star; the Prince is infatuated with American singer/dancer Karen O'Kane who performs "Begin the Beguine" (page 12); and the Princess has her eye on a renaissance man of the theater. "Just One of Those Things" is sung near the end of the second act by the Prince and Karen O'Kane as they fall, fatefully, out of love. Countless artists have recorded "Just One of Those Things" including Doris Day, Peggy Lee, Frank Sinatra, Diana Krall, Oscar Peterson, and Nat "King" Cole.

Words and Music by Cole Porter
Arranged by Dan Coates

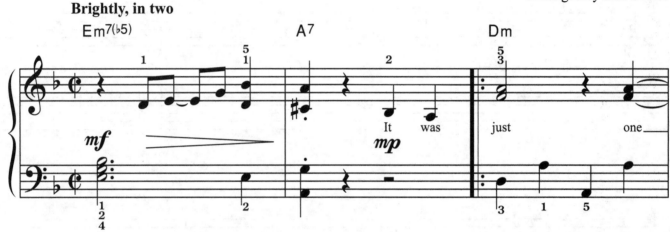

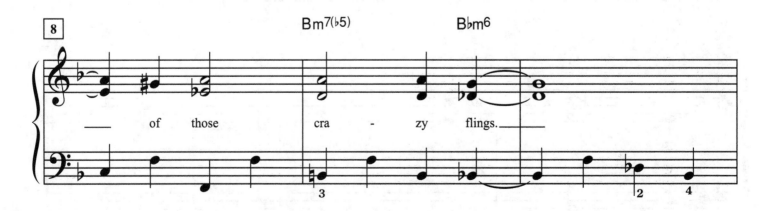

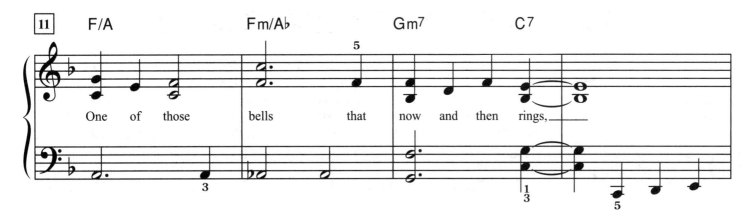

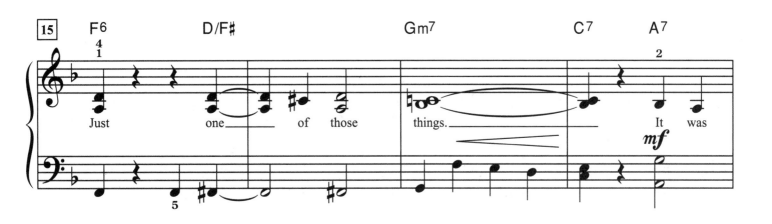

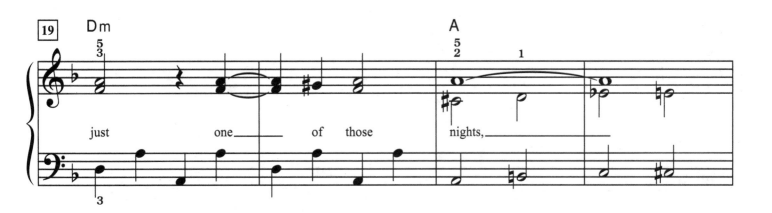

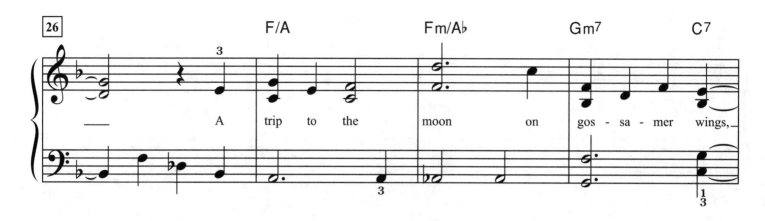

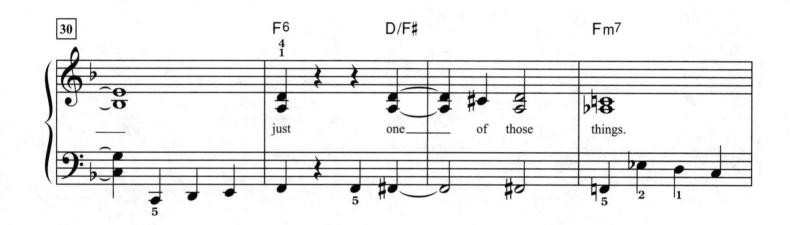

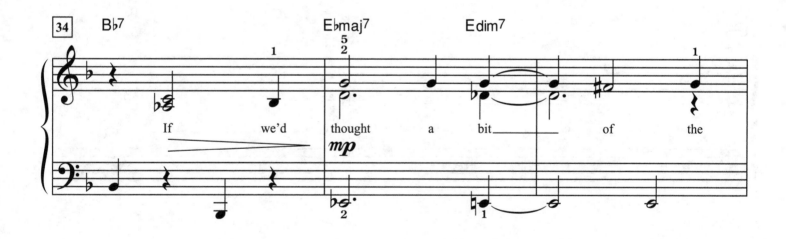

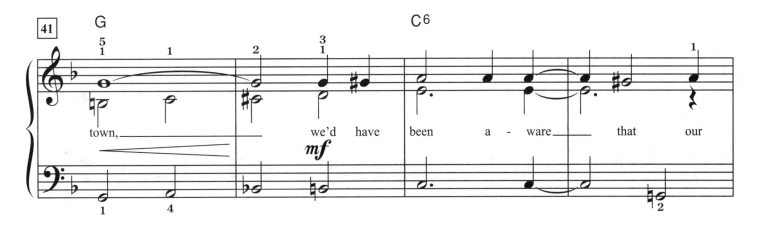

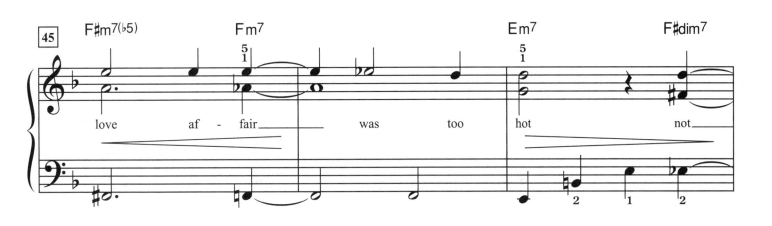

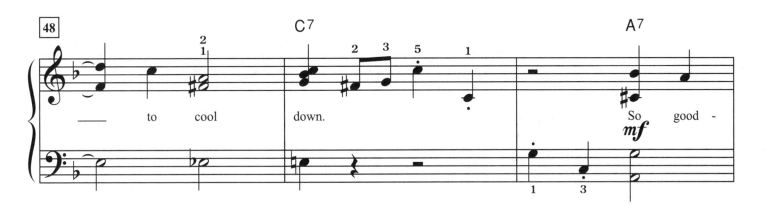

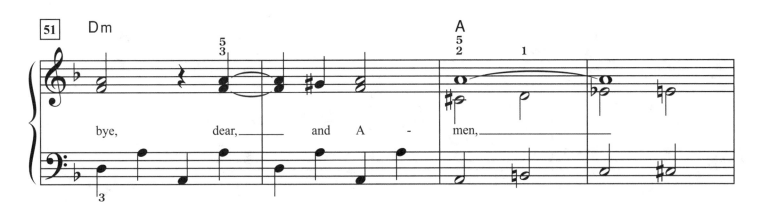

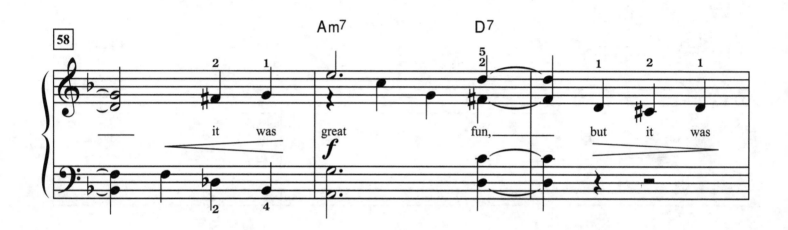

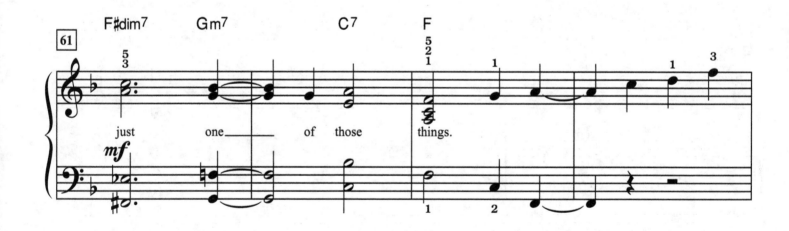

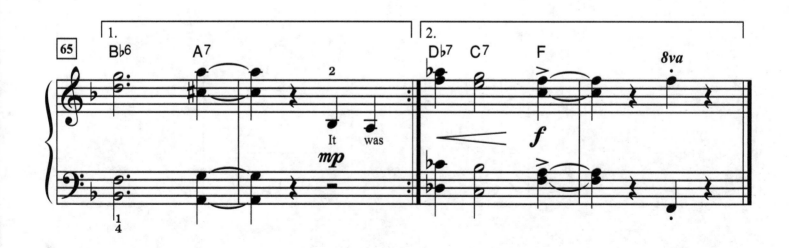

THE LADY IS A TRAMP

Along with "My Funny Valentine" (page 121) and "Where or When" (page 138), "The Lady Is a Tramp" is from the 1937 musical *Babes in Arms.* Many singers from different decades have put their spin on this classic song that spoofs high society: Tommy Dorsey in the 1930s, Frank Sinatra in the 1940s, and Ella Fitzgerald in the 1950s, to name a few.

Words by Lorenz Hart
Music by Richard Rodgers
Arranged by Dan Coates

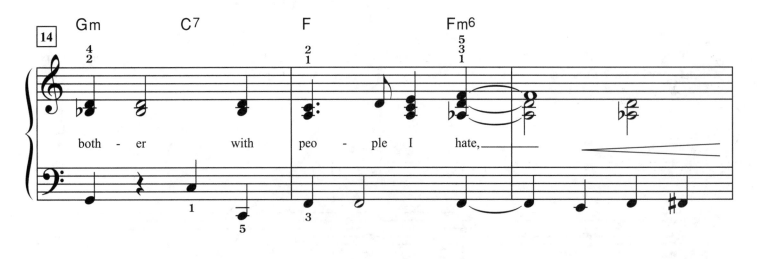

both - er with peo - ple I hate,

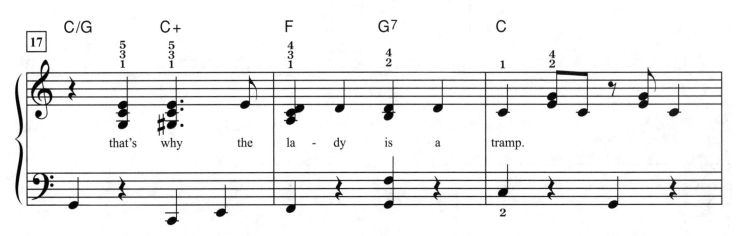

that's why the la - dy is a tramp.

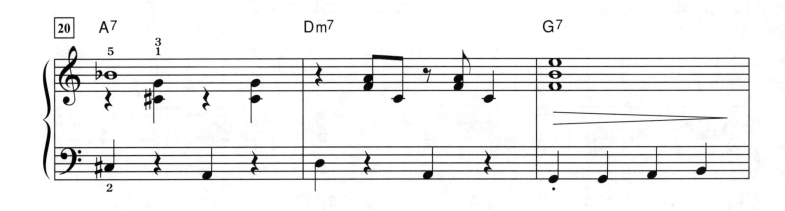

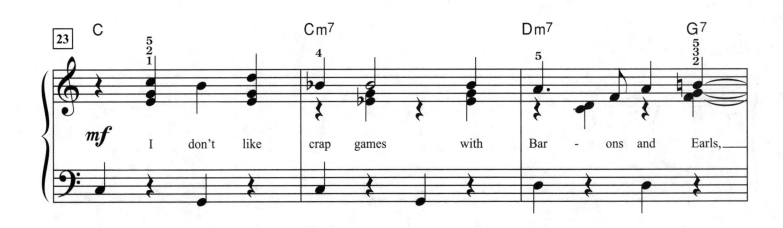

mf I don't like crap games with Bar - ons and Earls,

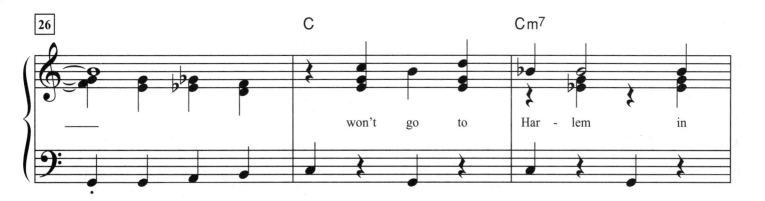

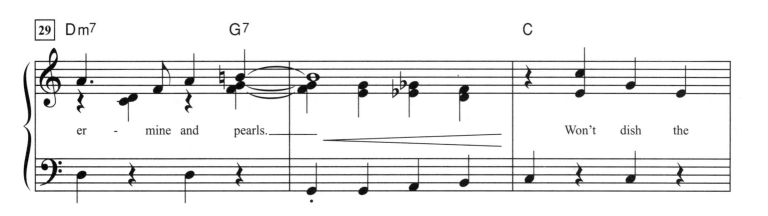

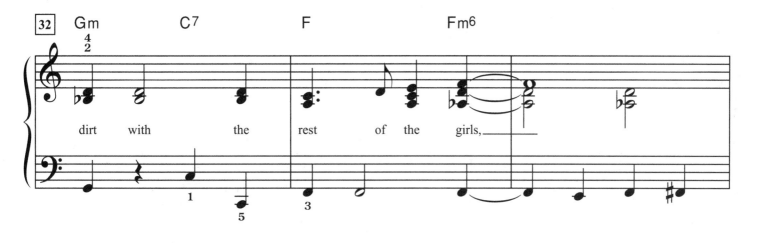

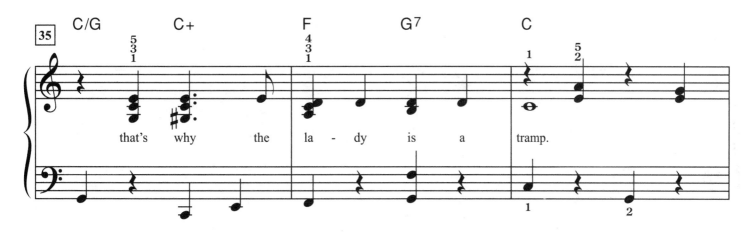

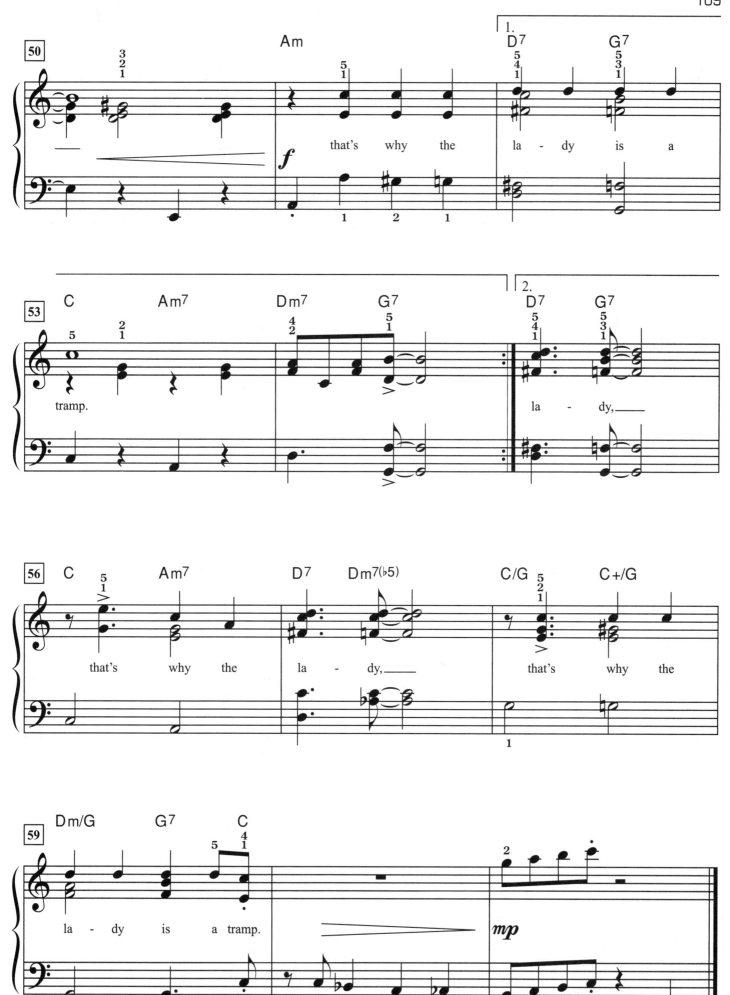

LET'S CALL THE WHOLE THING OFF

"Let's Call the Whole Thing Off" was first sung by Fred Astaire and Ginger Rogers in the 1937 film *Shall We Dance*. The famed duo performed the song while on roller skates. While *Shall We Dance* was the seventh Astaire and Rogers collaboration, it was the first Hollywood musical film that featured a score written by George and Ira Gershwin.

Music and Lyrics by
George Gershwin and Ira Gershwin
Arranged by Dan Coates

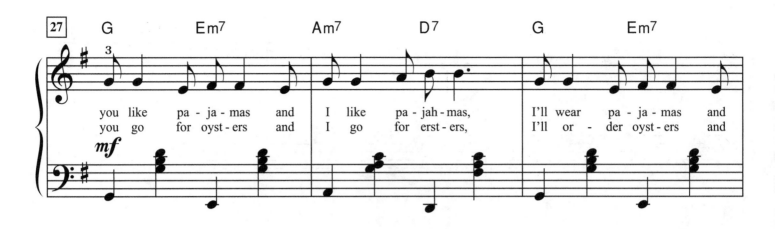

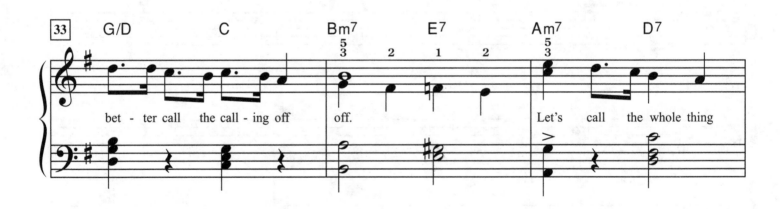

LOVE FOR SALE

"Love for Sale" was originally written for the 1930 musical *The New Yorkers.* Although the song was initially met with criticism for being written from the perspective of a prostitute, it became a chart-topping hit for artists in the 1930s and beyond. Just a few of the singers who have put their spin on "Love for Sale" include Tony Bennett, Harry Connick Jr., Elvis Costello, Ella Fitzgerald, Billie Holiday, The Manhattan Transfer, and Mel Tormé.

Words and Music by Cole Porter
Arranged by Dan Coates

Moderately slow

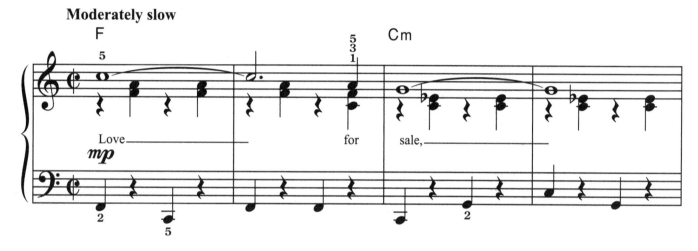

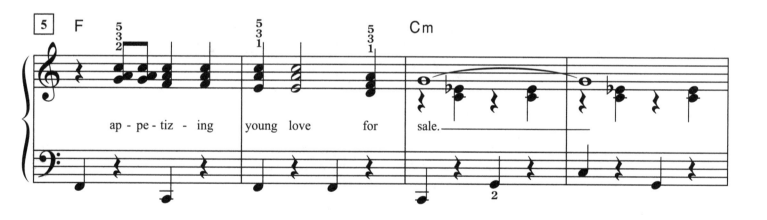

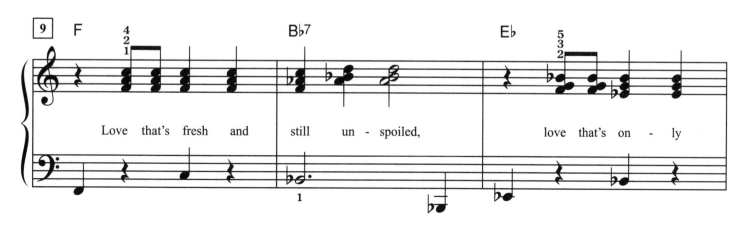

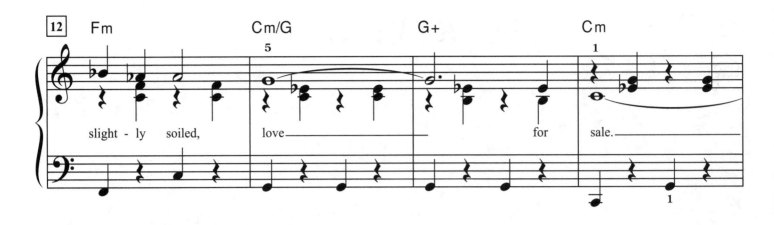

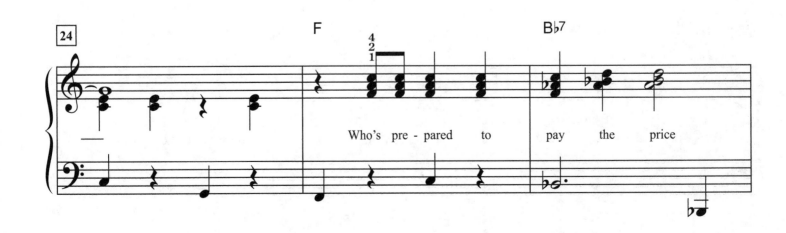

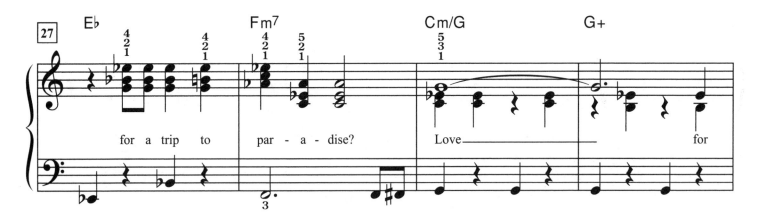

for a trip to par - a - dise? Love _____ for

sale. _____ *mp* Let the po - ets pipe of love

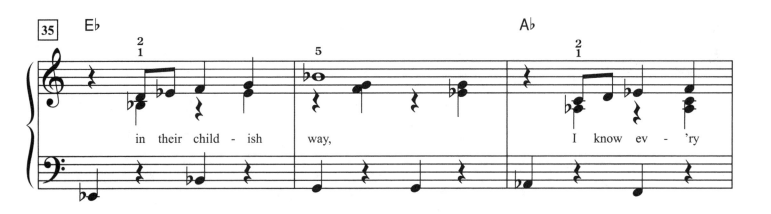

in their child - ish way, I know ev - 'ry

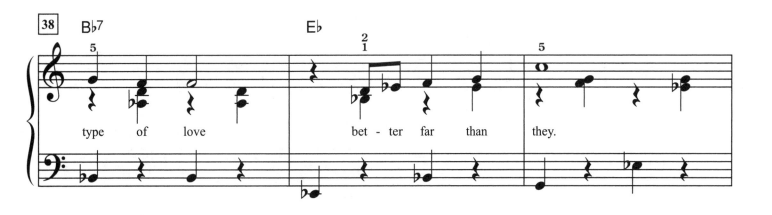

type of love bet - ter far than they.

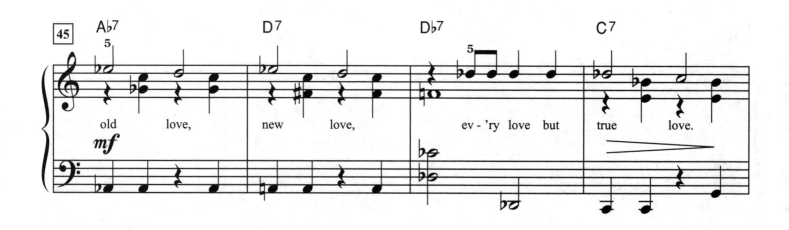

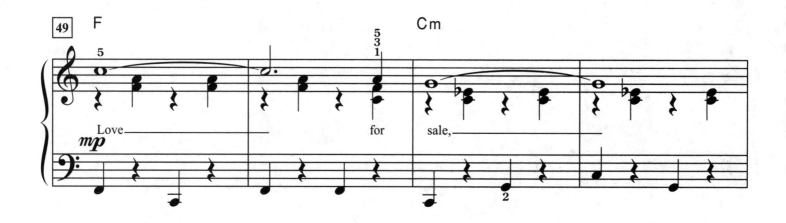

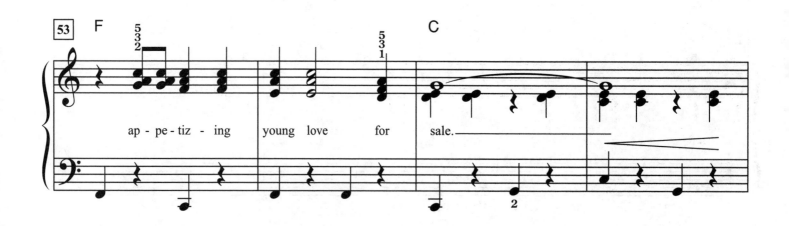

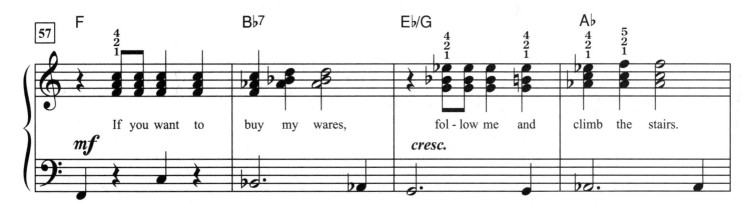

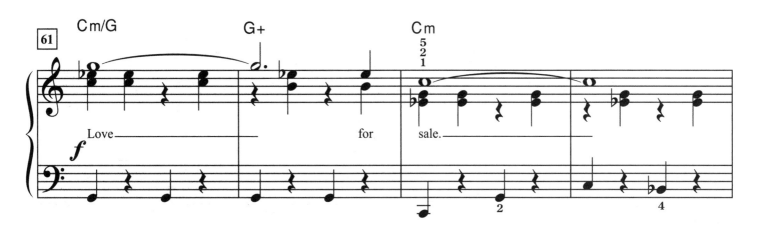

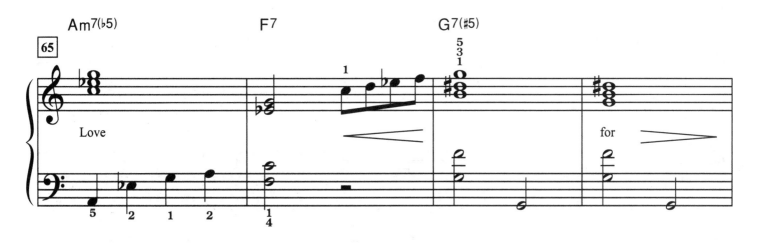

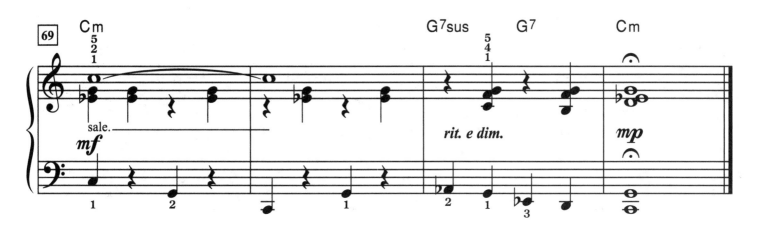

LULLABY OF BROADWAY

"Lullaby of Broadway" was introduced in the musical film *Gold Diggers of 1935*, one of many money-making movies in Warner Bros. *Gold Diggers* series of films. The song inspired a 1951 movie, *Lullaby of Broadway*, which starred Doris Day. However, it is widely known for its use in the popular musical *42nd Street*, which featured many classic songs by Harry Warren and Al Dubin.

Words by Al Dubin
Music by Harry Warren
Arranged by Dan Coates

MY FUNNY VALENTINE

"My Funny Valentine"—another hit song from *Babes in Arms* (see "Where or When" on page 138)—has been recorded by countless artists: Barbra Streisand, Ella Fitzgerald, Frank Sinatra, Tony Bennett, Buddy Rich, Mel Tormé, Sammy Davis Jr., Stan Getz, Sarah Vaughan, Anita O'Day, and many others. Perhaps the most influential recording was a collaboration made in 1953 by the Gerry Mulligan Quartet and Chet Baker, a jazz trumpeter and velvet-voiced singer. This recording featured a memorable solo by Baker and soared to the top of the charts.

Words by Lorenz Hart
Music by Richard Rodgers
Arranged by Dan Coates

NIGHT AND DAY

"Night and Day" is one of Cole Porter's most popular compositions. It was originally written for his 1932 musical *Gay Divorce*, which starred Fred Astaire. More Americans were introduced to "Night and Day" through Astaire's performance of it in the film version of the musical, which was re-named *The Gay Divorcée*. In addition to Astaire, other singers including Frank Sinatra, Ella Fitzgerald, Ringo Starr, and U2 have all put their spin on this classic.

Words and Music by Cole Porter
Arranged by Dan Coates

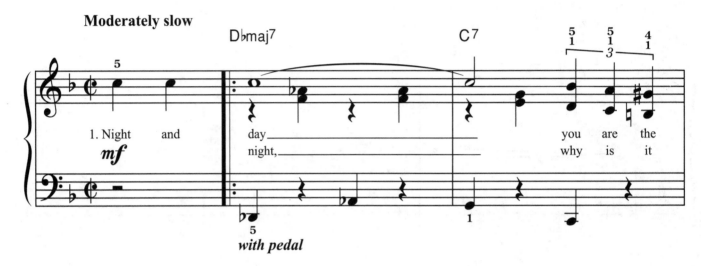

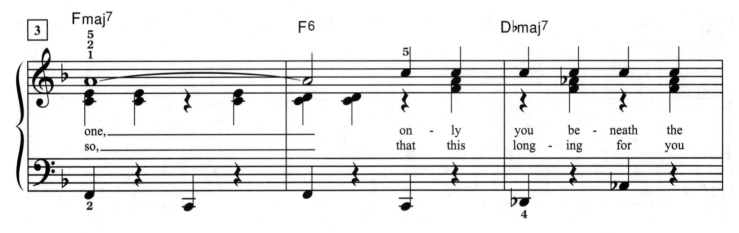

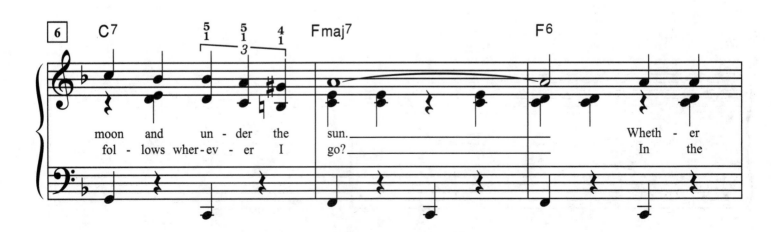

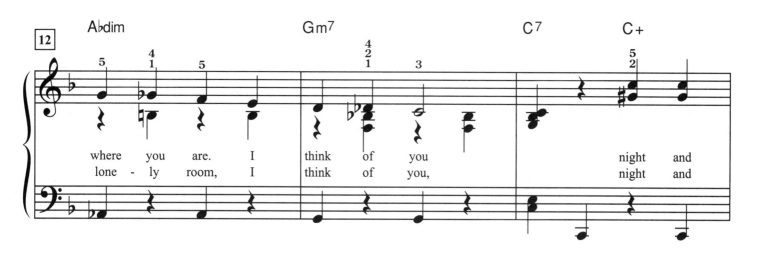

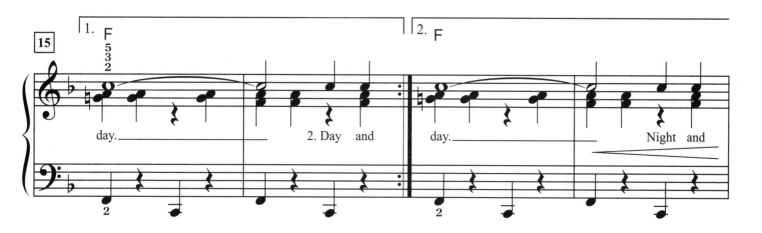

there's an oh, such a hun - gry yearn - ing, burn - ing in -

side of me._____ And its tor - ment won't be

through 'til you let me spend my life mak - ing love to you,

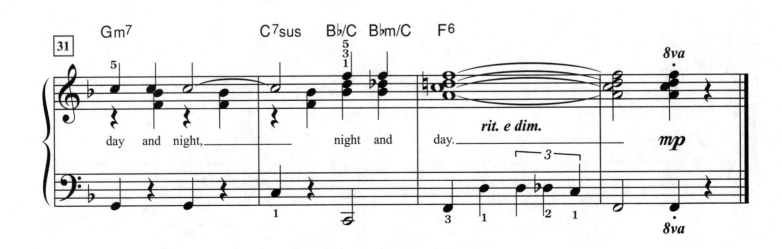

day and night,_____ night and day._____

PENNIES FROM HEAVEN

"Pennies from Heaven" was first introduced by legendary Bing Crosby in the 1936 movie of the same name. Writers Arthur Johnston and Johnny Burke received an Oscar nomination that year for Best Original Song, and multiple recordings by popular artists soon followed. Frank Sinatra, Louis Armstrong, Tony Bennett, Dean Martin, Dave Brubeck, and others have since recorded this hit.

Words by Johnny Burke
Music by Arthur Johnston
Arranged by Dan Coates

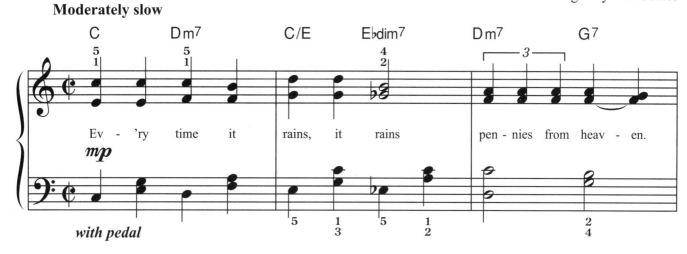

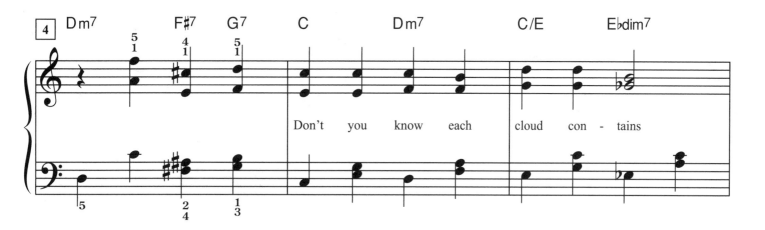

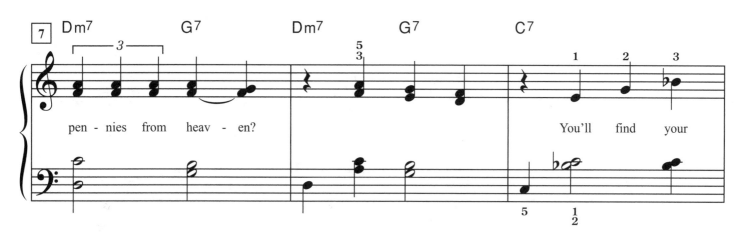

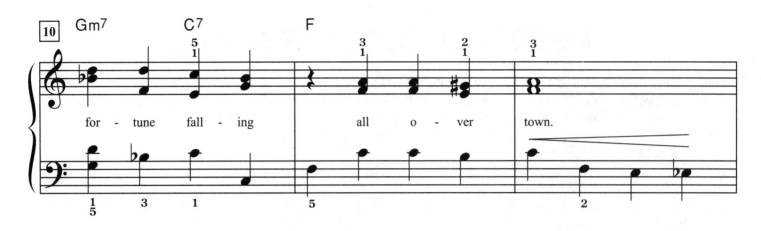

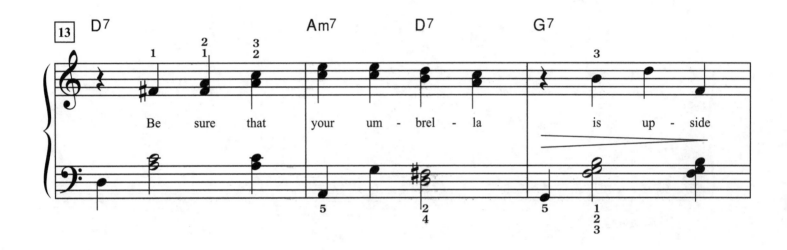

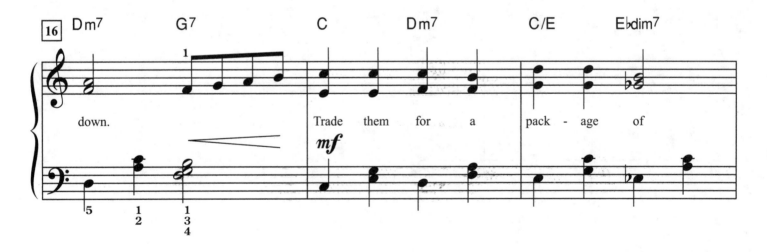

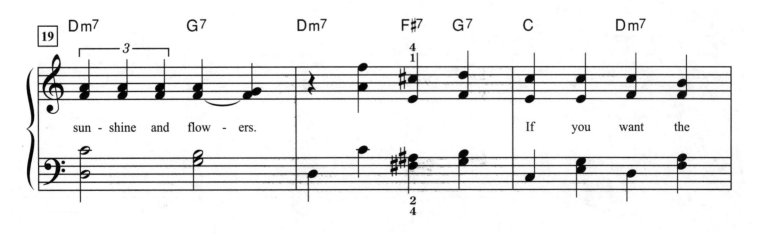

SUMMERTIME

"Summertime" was originally written as an aria for the opera *Porgy and Bess*. In the opera, it is one of the first arias and is sung as a lullaby. The song has since become a staple, not only in the world of opera but also in pop and jazz. Many renditions have made their way into the mainstream by artists such as Janis Joplin, Billie Holiday, and Nina Simone. There is also a famous collaborative recording by Ella Fitzgerald and Louis Armstrong.

Music and Lyrics by George Gershwin,
DuBose and Dorothy Heyward and Ira Gershwin
Arranged by Dan Coates

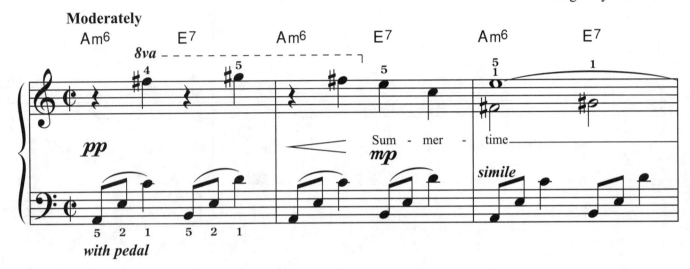

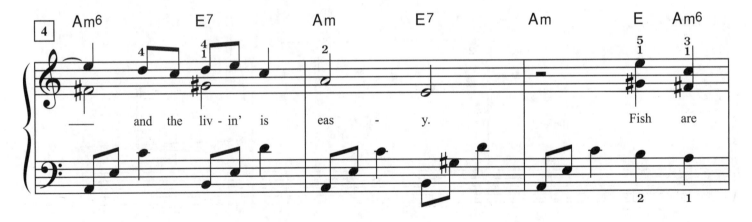

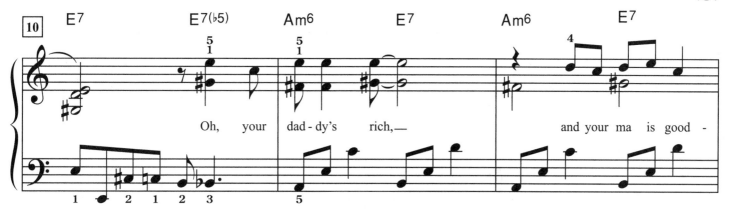

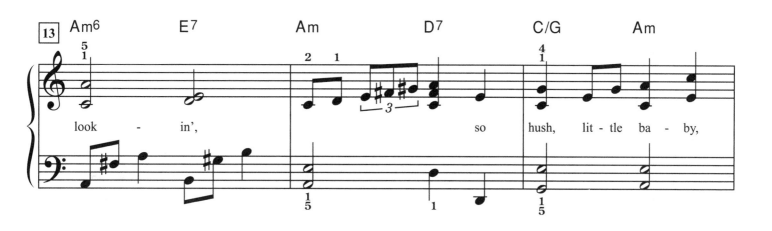

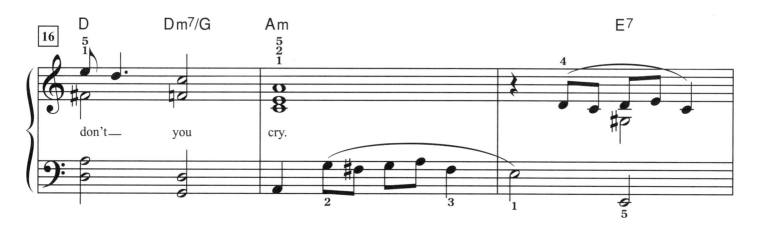

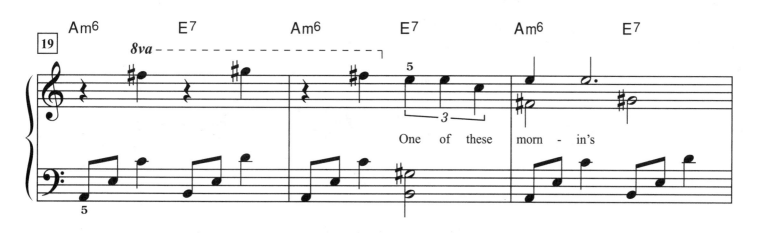

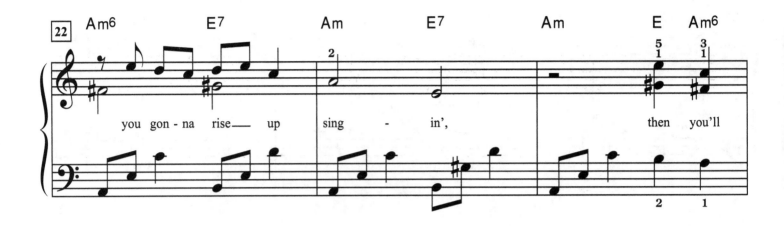

you gon-na rise—— up sing - in', then you'll

spread your wings and you'll take to the sky.

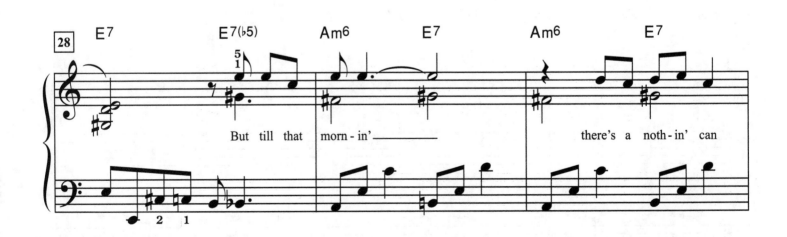

But till that morn-in'———— there's a noth-in' can

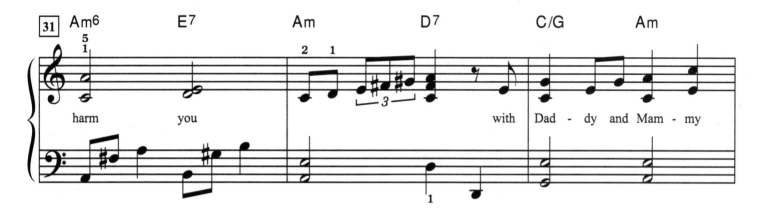

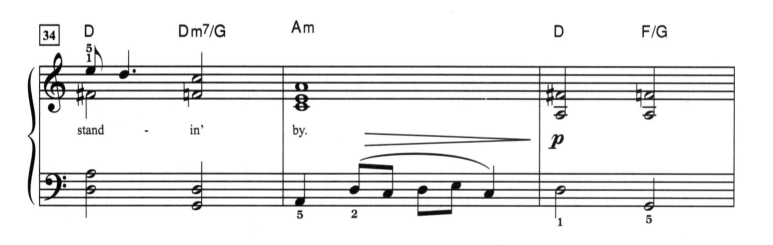

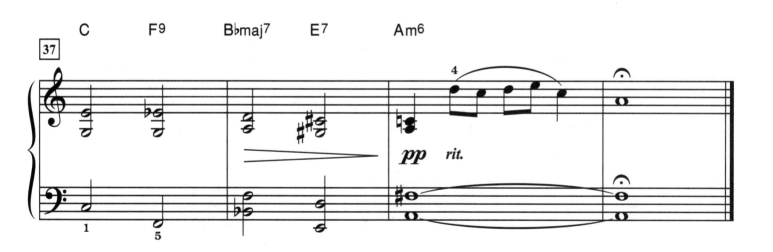

WHAT A DIFF'RENCE A DAY MADE

Though it was written in 1934, the most famous recording of this classic song is by Dinah Washington, who won a Grammy in 1959 for her quintessential interpretation. A staple of the Great American Songbook, its lyrics were originally written in Spanish by the Mexican composer María Méndez Grever. The Spanish influence can be heard in the bolero style maintained in most versions of the tune.

Music and Spanish Words by María Grever
English Words by Stanley Adams
Arranged by Dan Coates

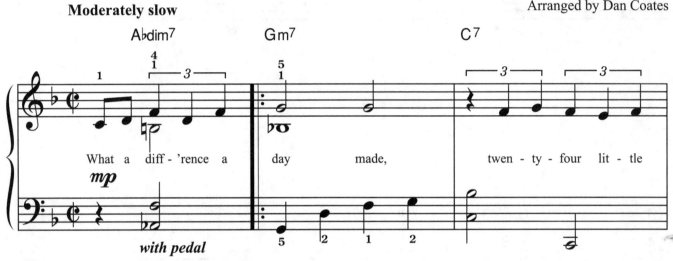

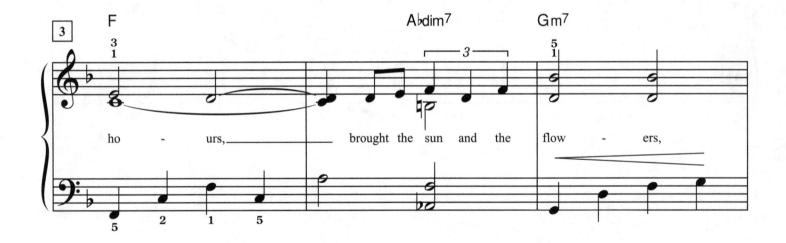

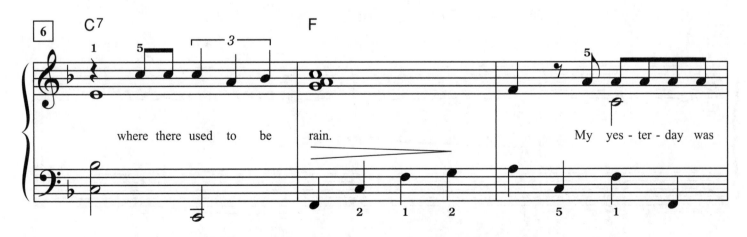

136

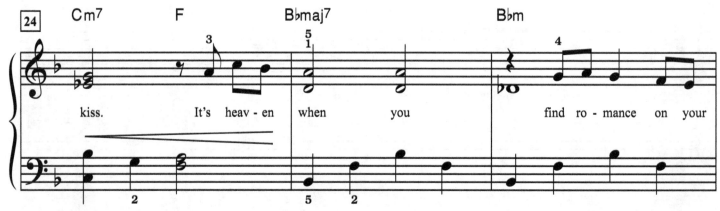

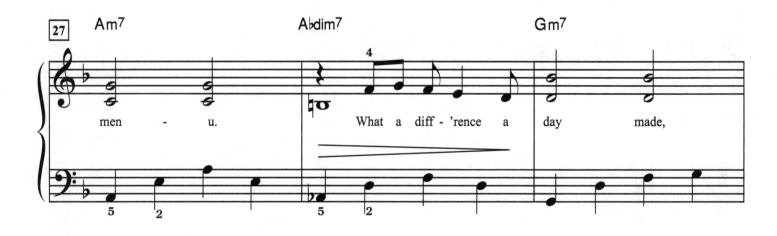

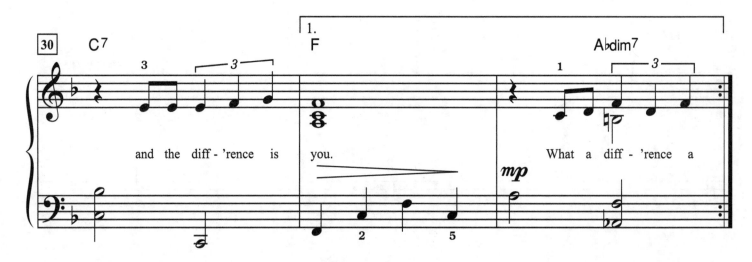

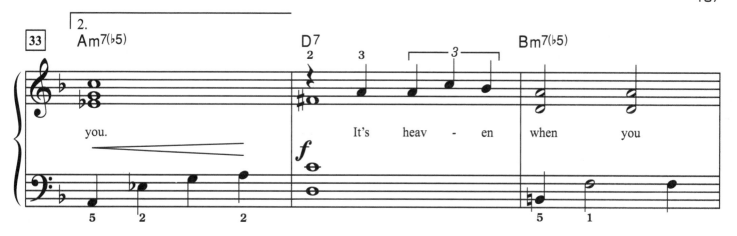

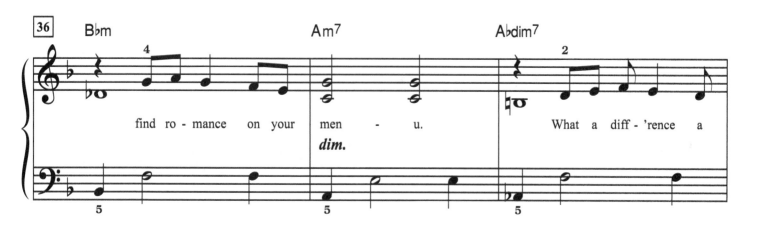

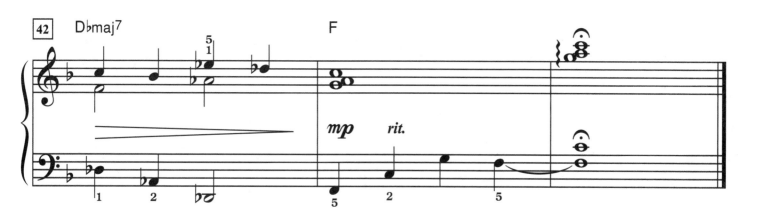

WHERE OR WHEN

"Where or When" was written for the 1937 Rodgers and Hart musical *Babes in Arms,* which featured many hit songs: "My Funny Valentine" (page 121), "The Lady Is a Tramp" (page 105), "Johnny One Note," and "I Wish I Were In Love Again." In 1939, the musical was made into a successful movie starring Mickey Rooney, who was nominated for an Oscar for his performance, and Judy Garland, who had just finished filming *The Wizard of Oz.*

Words by Lorenz Hart
Music by Richard Rodgers
Arranged by Dan Coates

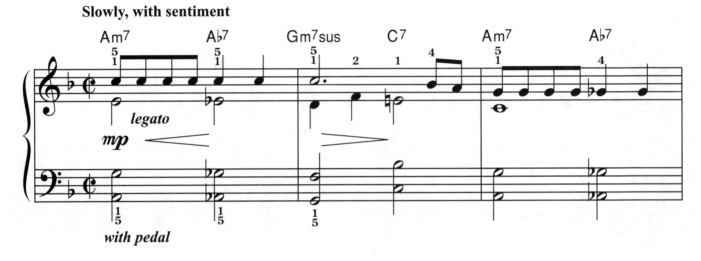

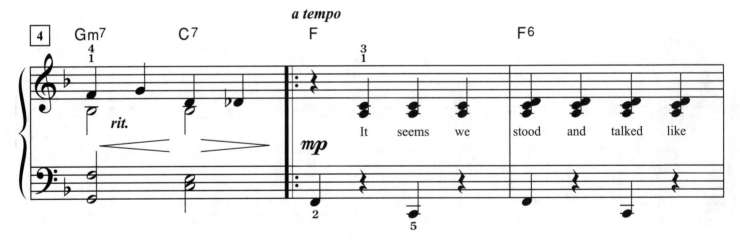

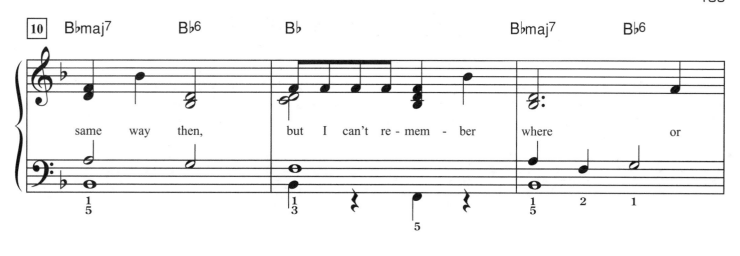

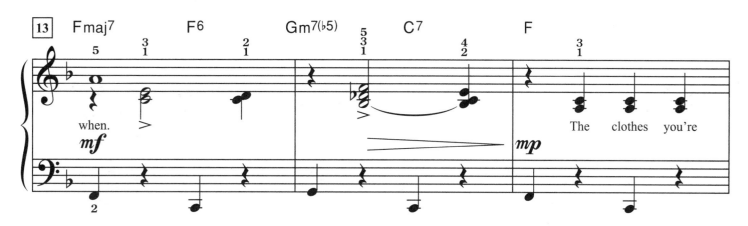

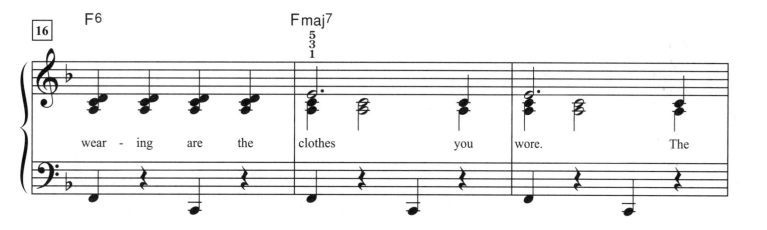

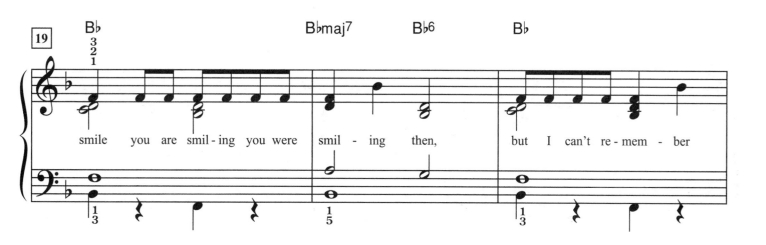

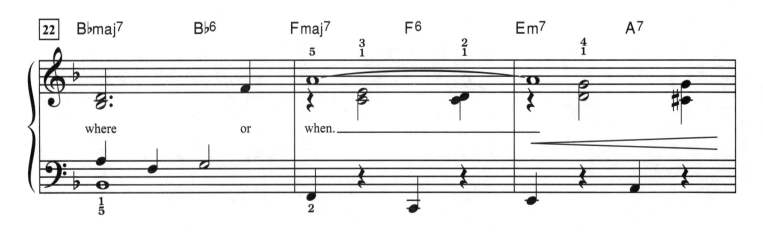

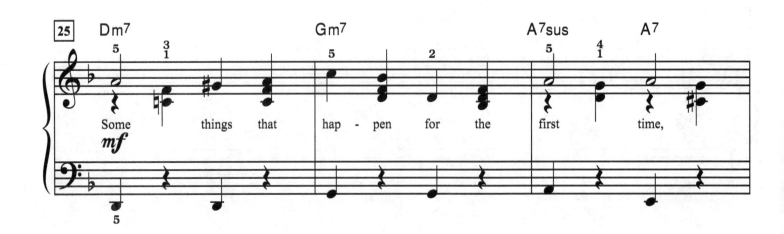

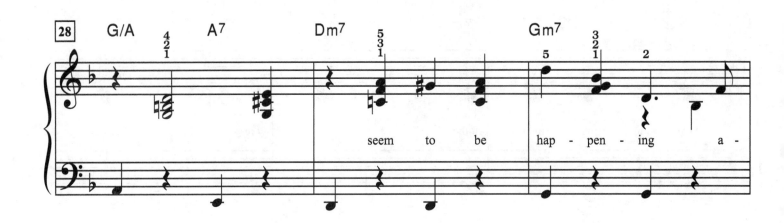

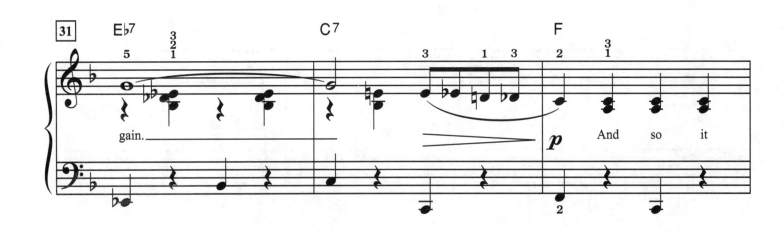

YOU OUGHTA BE IN PICTURES

Dana Suesse, the composer of "You Oughta Be in Pictures," was at one time labeled "the girl Gershwin." She studied with the famous composition teacher Nadia Boulanger, and her impressive career included collaborations with lyricist Eddie Heyman, band leader Paul Whiteman, impresario Billy Rose, and many others. Suesse's works have been performed at Carnegie Hall, at the Newport Music Festival, and in countless concert halls around the world.

Words by Edward Heyman
Music by Dana Suesse
Arranged by Dan Coates

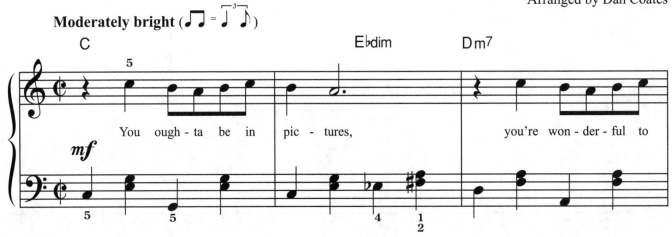

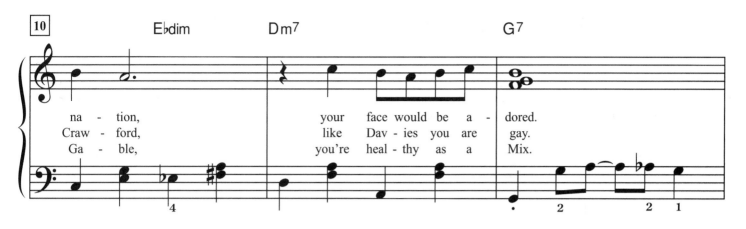

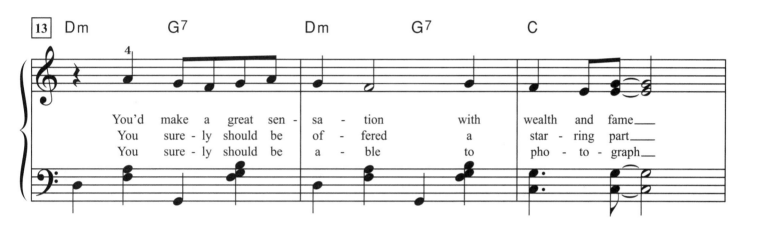

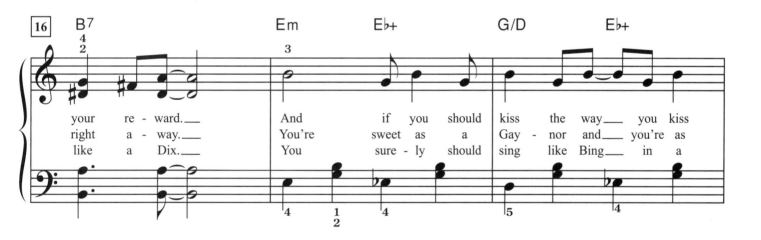

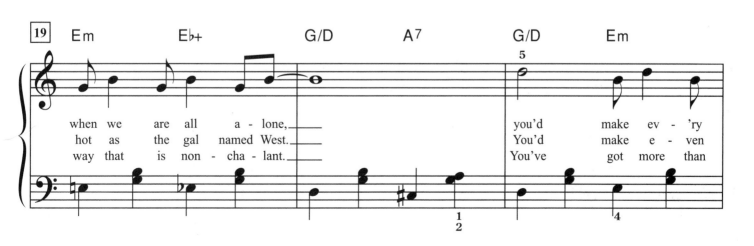